AND
PONIES

Text by
Caroline Silver

Illustrations by
Christine Bousfield

HarperCollins*Publishers*

First published 1988

© in the text Caroline Silver 1988
© in the illustrations Christine Bousfield 1988

ISBN 0 00 458869 X

Colour reproduction by Adroit Photo-Litho Ltd, Birmingham
Filmset by Wordsmiths, London
Printed and bound in Great Britain by
HarperCollins*Manufacturing*, Glasgow

10 9 8 7 6 5 4 3

Contents

The evolution of the horse

The horse dates back 30 million years further than man. Its earliest form, *Hyracotherium*, looked nothing like a modern horse. It stood about 30cm (12in) tall, had four toes on its forefeet and three on its hind, and looked faintly like a fox terrier.

It is fairly certain, from the vast numbers of fossilized bones found in the southern United States, that *Hyracotherium* originated in that part of the world, and there is also evidence that, before the Bering Strait split the Far West from the Far East, it wandered across into Asia and Europe.

Hyracotherium is more commonly called *Eohippus*, meaning 'the dawn horse'. It was last seen alive on this earth – although not by man, who had not yet evolved – some 40 million years ago. It was succeeded by *Orohippus* and *Epihippus*, animals with very similar skeletal structure but with more efficient teeth. These gave way, over the next 15 million years, to the bigger *Mesohippus* and *Miohippus*, which could browse on soft plants and which had started to carry their weight on the central toe of what had, by now, become three-toed feet, and *Merychippus*, with longer grinding teeth.

Pliohippus, of the Lower Pliocene age, was the first fully-hooved horse. It stood entirely on its central toe of three, with its toenail developed into a wall of hoof. It looked reasonably like a horse and, by the time that

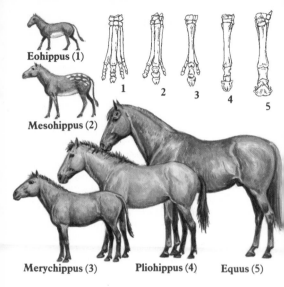

Eohippus (1)

Mesohippus (2)

Merychippus (3) **Pliohippus (4)** **Equus (5)**

homo sapiens first appeared, it had developed further into *Equus* and had grown to over 120cm (4ft) high.

Relics of *Equus* suggest that, like the dawn horse, it originated in North America. It migrated south-ward, to become South America's earliest horse, and also wandered to Asia, Europe and Africa. About 8000 years ago it became extinct as a recognisable type, but its progeny in Europe, Africa and Asia, adapted in little ways to suit varying climate and terrain, became the ancestors of the modern horse.

Three basic types of *Equus*, the Steppe, the Forest and the Plateau horses of prehistory, developed into the huge variety of *Equus caballus* that is known today.

The **Steppe** type, which is still seen in Przewalski's Horse (*page 178*), had a large head with long ears, a long face and a convex profile. It had a short, strong body, slender limbs, narrow hooves and a mane which stood up like a brush on a thick neck. It was alert and agile, which is doubtless why it still survives.

The **Forest** type was heavier than the Steppe and duller witted. It was a thickly-built horse with hooves broad enough to support it on marshy ground. Its head was broad and short, concave between the eyes and convex towards the muzzle, which helped it to browse on eye-level shoots. It had a thick, hairy coat, often with spots or stripes which merged it into the dappled shadows in which it lived. It was frightened of water, no doubt because predators lurked in the trees surrounding forest drinking places. It is now extinct, but its successors live on in today's kindly, unimaginative heavy horses.

The **Plateau** type, very probably the ancestor of our finer-boned horses and ponies, may still exist in the few remaining herds of Tarpan (*page 198*). These animals have small, narrow heads with small ears and large eyes, lightweight bodies and long, slim limbs.

The shape of their hooves lies between the long narrowness of the Steppe and the broad roundness of the Forest horses. These horses are thought to be the ancestors of today's lightweight horse and pony breeds.

Most horses have come a very long way from the three primitive types and the modern breeds did not evolve by themselves. They were purpose-bred by man for selected qualities such as speed, robustness, strength, agility or beauty. So many breeds of horse exist today that it is sometimes hard to tell one from another.

Types of horse

The following *types* are not breeds, in so much as that both parents were of similar heredity, but are physical types which could result from random breeding.

COB

The Cob is a stocky, weight-carrying small horse or large pony, ranging in height from 14 hands to 15.2 hands (1 hand = 4in or 10cm, *see Glossary*), suited to temperate climates, and of an intelligent, calm and amiable temper.

HACK

The Hack, which could be considered a horse of the past if it were not still much-prized in horse-show classes, was the ideal exercise mount of the fashionable lady. It is a smallish, elegant horse, not more than 15.3 hands high; a lightweight, slim-legged aristocrat of a subdued colour such as bay, brown or black (though chestnut and grey are acceptable) with perfect manners and smooth paces.

Prize-winning hacks in Europe are usually small Thoroughbreds, whereas in North America they are preponderantly Saddlebreds. In both cases they are charming, lightweight saddle horses.

SHOW PONY

The Show Pony is a child-sized Hack. For the benefit of children small to large, it comes in three sizes: up to 12.2 hands high, up to 13.2 hands high, and up to 14.2 hands.

It is judged on its physical beauty, on its manners (which should be calm and confident, as befits an animal which will carry a young rider) and on its smoothness and elegance of movement at the walk, the trot and the canter. Refinement of physique and slimness of outline are much admired in this type of pony. Prizewinners usually carry Welsh or Thoroughbred bloodlines.

EVENTER

The Eventer is a strong, sound, intelligent horse. It must be obedient enough to shine on the dressage test - the first phase of a three-day event which tests the horses's harmony with its rider. It must be bold enough to survive the 27-odd km (17-odd miles) of the second phase, the endurance phase which tests both its stamina and its cross-country jumping ability. It must be brave and physically strong enough to complete the third phase of show jumping, despite being stiff and sore after its endurance test.

Eventers come in all shapes and sizes. The optimum is just over 16 hands high and, because of the speed neeeded to pass the endurance test without time penalties, the breeding is usually Thoroughbred or near Thoroughbred.

DRESSAGE HORSE

Any horse or pony of good physique and tractable temperament, given a skilled rider, is capable of learning dressage, and there are no standards to say that this or that sort of animal may not compete in this exacting sport. But to succeed at top level the Dressage Horse should be a big, imposing animal exuding personal presence and should not be of a colour (for example skewbald or spotted) to distract the eye from the movement of the horse as a whole.

Successful dressage horses are usually bay, brown or chestnut, standing 16-18 hands high, and are often of Carriage Horse type. Naturally good movement is essential. Dutch and German horses, such as Hanoverians and Oldenburgers, are most popular, with Thoroughbred blood for extra grace and fire.

SHOW JUMPER

The Show Jumper comes in every size and shape. There is no known way of breeding a horse which will happily leap over huge obstacles in cold blood. Consistently good ones must be sound of wind and limb, and usually have large backsides to generate power of jump.

But there are also little, slippy horses which can turn on a sixpence in speed competitions and spring like cats in Olympic classes.

Top-class show jumpers give everything they have to jump unjumpable obstacles, often higher than their heads. They delight in their prowess and relish applause for their work. The best go on long past the usual age of retirement for a horse.

POLO PONY

The Polo Pony is a fast, quick-thinking and quick-turning animal, usually about 15 hands high (and so it is, strictly speaking, a horse rather than a

pony). Breed is immaterial, though most of the best are Criollos or small Thoroughbreds.

Very good polo ponies are prima donnas and enjoy praise from their audience. The best play polo better than most of their riders.

RACEHORSE

The Racehorse, if a star, will give his all to get his nose in front at the winning post. Most racehorses are Thoroughbreds which have been bred for speed, but it is not always so.

Horses have been tested for speed for more than 5000 years – for about 4800 years before the Thoroughbred was evolved. Very early forms of

racing, such as those practised by the Hittites, involved making horses extremely thirsty and then loosing them to see which would be first to reach the water.

Modern racing includes trotting racing, Quarter Horse racing, Arab racing and even – in America – Shetland Pony racing. As long as horses can be matched for speed, man will always gamble on the outcome.

HUNTER

The Hunter is simply a horse suited to foxhunting. It must be powerful enough to carry a rider all day long. For show purposes hunters are grouped as lightweights (which will carry up to 79kg/175lbs), middle-weights (up to 89kg/196lbs) and heavyweights (over 89kg/196lbs). There are also small hunters (14.2-15.2 hands high) and ladies' hunters (very lightweight).

Good hunters are brave, intelligent and obedient. Physically, the variety is enormous. Horses which wade over ploughed land need to be broad-hooved and sturdy, those which trick along hillside country need to be nimble and iron-lunged, and those which run over flatter grassland need to be swift and able to jump on the run.

COACH AND CARRIAGE HORSES

Combined Driving, now becoming a popular sport, uses the most nimble and intelligent of the four-in-hand Coach horse types which, a century ago, were used to haul coach-loads of passengers over unmade roads. Modern needs being recreational and sportive, these horses often lack the physique of the heftier carriage horses of times gone by.

Strongly-built Carriage Horses are still used for traditional ceremonies, such as the procession to and from the State Opening of the British Parliament, but these horses are chosen – and carefully trained – more for their calm ability to ignore crowd pressures than for their strength to pull today's increasingly-light carriages.

COLDBLOODS

The massive power of the many derivatives from the original Forest type of horse, nowadays called Coldblood, may make us question what we do when we refine an animal specifically for human purposes and then, because of some invention of our technology, take away that animal's purpose.

Today's heavy horses were selectively bred by man over the past 1000 years. Originally they were bred to bear the enormous weight of an armoured knight: these horses were not as tall, nor as strong, as the big Coldbloods of today, but nonetheless they were the 'Great Horses' of the middle ages. Because of their size they were slow and unwieldy, with the result that their riders were beaten in battle when confronted by less-constricted armies on smaller and more manoeuvrable horses.

These Great Horse gentle giants of the middle ages were then bred to become even bigger and stronger. For the last five centuries or so they have pulled ploughs through unyielding ground, hauled huge tree trunks through the forest undergrowth and carted heavy loads of every kind. Teams of heavy horses are still seen in parts of North America, often pulling combine harvesters. Small wonder that the word 'horsepower' has become a respected measure of strength.

Though the day of the carthorse is largely over, it is still used in countries which are too rugged or too cold for motor vehicles. Some are still bred for pleasure and the most handsome of these have become status symbols for the very brewery companies for which their ancestors once worked.

The care and management of horses

Horse sense

Good horsemen understand a horse's viewpoint. They know what will upset it, and what will reassure it. It would be nice to say, conversely, that a trusty horse knows the mind of its master; but this only happens in the cases of very perceptive masters. Most riders are conditioned to human signals – for example, a red light means stop – and often do not realize that horses have a different, more basic, set of guidelines.

Domestic horses, no matter how cossetted, retain the natural instincts of the wild. Fear predominates: the wild horse survives by shying clear of cover which might harbour an attacker – and this includes small cover, such as a drifting paper bag. If in doubt, shy away; if alarmed, run away fast. If a predator sits on your back, buck him off (not to be confused with bucking from *joie de vivre*). Man may feel that the horse exists to carry a rider, but no one told the horse that this is so.

In dealing with fear, and indeed at all times, the handling of horses should be kind and positive. Instructions need to be given clearly and patiently. Sharp voices and sudden movements should be avoided. All horses respond to a gentle flow of nonsense chat. They also respond to an arm, slid quietly over the neck, which leans down heavily on the mane. It feels to them similar to the natural soothing gesture of one horse resting its head on another's neck.

Herd instinct is another dominant characteristic. Horses, like humans, live in tribes, depending on each other for company and reassurance. Horses who are asked to live alone, as many are today, understandably become lonely and tense. Even the best riding school horse becomes jumpy and baulky when separated from his companions. Horses – like humans – need friends around and, failing another horse, a donkey, goat or cow will make a lonely paddock more bearable.

There is much harm done by well-meaning people who think its own fenced acre of grass is paradise to a horse. It isn't!

Horses like regular routines and are easily upset by change. Any horse moved to a new home needs a week or two to settle down, just as a human does. A good owner will determine the former routine of a newly-purchased horse and will make gradual changes to convert it to his new routine before asking the horse to work. Horses respond to routine and are comforted to know that certain things will assuredly happen at the same time each day. So, if you want to make a horse feel comfortable, always feed him at, for instance, seven o'clock each morning, ride him at ten and catch him up from his paddock at four in the afternoon. If you don't keep to this routine he may wonder, as who would not, what surprise there is in store.

Horses learn by association. Their memories of unkind or startling occurrences remain with them from birth. Good horsemen know that a horse's background is usually different from their own and may be reasonable ground for odd behaviour. Making a horse move home, by buying it, is akin to moving a kindergarten child to a different sort of school with new parents and a new home. Memories remain in the child, or the horse – but in the horses's case he is much more concerned about horse life than human life. Horses associate with horse things and it is stupid of humans to expect them not to do so.

Horses, like humans, each have a different personality. Most horses will indicate their moods by conventional signs - but this is not always so. If you feel you want to jump away from a friendly-looking horse, then do – humans have instincts too!

Care of the horse at grass

Horses fed solely on grass need about three acres per head year-round, one acre (0.405 hectares) to be fenced for present use and the other two to be 'rested' to grow. Ponies, given good land in a temperate climate, can live off one acre per head.

Ideally three paddocks should be used in turn for one-third to two-thirds of a year on a one- or two-year cycle, which allows unused pasture to recover and for a hay crop to be cut for food for winter months.

Horses are wasteful grazers, stripping the best bits of pasture and using the worst as a lavatory area. Rotation grazing with cattle keeps all the grass evenly cropped and prevents the pasture from becoming 'horse sick' with parasitic worms in the rank, uneaten parts. If cattle are not available, either gather the horse droppings daily or brush-harrow regularly to disperse them and cut the weeds down with a gang mower.

Fencing needs regular inspection. A horse can walk through a weak point in a hedge, or damage itself on sagging barbed wire. Gates must be wide enough for an excited horse to bustle through, and fastened securely against inquisitive horses.

A horse needs shelter: a windbreak and shade from hot summer sun. Tall hedges or trees may suffice but the best solution is a roofed, three-sided shelter with its back against the coldest wind.

All horses need fresh water. If there is not a clear stream running through the field, the best provision is a self-filling tank on a mains water suppy. Failing this, use an old tank or bath – but empty it and scrub it out at least once every week or the water will become stale.

Native ponies will survive the hardest winter without a stable, provided that their coats are left naturally long and shaggy and that the protective dust and mud is not groomed out of them. Stuffy, drafty stables are bad for them, causing coughs and colds, and they are healthier living outdoors – as, indeed, are most horses with thick winter coats; but, if you find them shivering, bring them in.

In the barren winter months a grass-fed horse or pony on restricted pasture needs as much hay as it

25

can eat. As grass dies down in autumn start with a quarter of a bale (about 5.5kg/14lbs) and feed more as the animal eats it up. Feed twice as much, and twice a day, when snow falls. A haynet, tied at the height of the horse's mouth and preferably under shelter, is economic both against rain damage and because the horse can't trample it. Working animals need oats or concentrated feed in the form of 'nuts' to supplement their hay.

Daily inspection of a horse's feet is sensible, both to remove damaging stones and to check the condition of the hoof and horseshoe. A horse without healthy feet cannot work. Most horses need new shoes every six weeks to protect their hooves from wear, but check with your farrier.

When the rich grass comes up in spring, horses

should be carefully watched. Native ponies, especially, are instinctively greedy because of millennia of grabbing food from lean pasture. Given rich grass, animals will stuff themselves and may make themselves seriously ill.

Good grazing requires a balance – horses do not live by grass alone. They need a mixture of 'weeds', which we might call 'herbs', to ensure a balanced diet. Brambles, dandelions and rosehips are all examples of good natural foods for horses. In the absence of mixed, well-balanced grazing a lump of rock salt will provide a horse with most of the minerals that it needs.

Some weeds are poisonous to horses. These will differ according to the area. Learn what they are and how to identify them, then inspect the pasture.

The stable

A stabled horse lives indoors for up to 23 hours a day, so the view from the stable is very important to him. He is happiest when there is plenty of activity to watch, especially if it involves other horses stabled nearby. Bored and lonely horses develop time-killing vices such as windsucking or weaving (*see Glossary of horse terms*), so visit the horse frequently and turn him out in the paddock whenever possible.

Stabled horses should be fed and watered three or four times a day, mucked out thoroughly at least once each day and regularly groomed to promote healthy circulation.

A feed bowl on the floor will suffice, though the horse may turn it over. If a fixed manger is used, make sure it is sited high enough to prevent the horse from getting his feet in it – but not so high that eating is difficult. Hay racks or nets should be at the horse's eye level, partly to avoid entangling its feet and partly to keep hayseeds out of its eyes. Water buckets should be scrubbed daily.

Stable floors should be waterproof, with a slight fall for drainage. To prevent flooding, they should be higher than external surroundings. A rough finish will guard against slipping. Cushion them with thick, clean bedding.

Good ventilation is essential. Half doors provide plenty of fresh air while protecting the body from drafts. Hopper windows give extra air and light. Set windows far back in walls or protect them with bars so that the horse cannot break them.

Outward-facing stable doors need overhanging eaves to protect the horse from sunstroke and from rain.

Stables should be built of a durable material. A horse will bake under a hot tin roof and can be kept awake by the noise of rain rattling upon it.

Looseboxes – stables in which the horse can wander about, as opposed to stalls in which he is tied by the head – are much the best accommodation. Their dimensions should be large enough to allow the horse to move freely and to avoid him being 'cast' (legs jammed up against a wall) when he rolls or lies down to sleep. A loosebox should be at least 3m/10ft square – the bigger the better – and should be no less than 2.4m/8ft high at the doorway, so that the horse does not bang his head, and rising to 3.6m/12ft inside for good air circulation.

Rows of stables are more interesting for a horse if partition walls allow him to see his neighbours from the inside. However, these walls need to be 4.8m/5ft high, to guard against kicking, and should have bars up to 2.4m/8ft to prevent biting. The siting of mangers is an art: finicky eaters will often eat better if they can feed competitively within sight of their neighbours.

Where many horses are kept, barn arrangements are popular. In these, horses live under the same roof and face each other across a central aisle, thus providing companionship and guarding against cold external winds. However, barns can give problems of ventilation and of condensation.

When building a stable it makes sense to ask advice from the veterinarian responsible for your horse's health.

Daily routine
Stabled horses need an hour or two of exercise every day. Old-fashioned practices left the horse indoors on Sundays, but this gave rise to a rigid muscular condition called 'Monday morning sickness' (azoturia). Horses who have been worked hard the previous day (hunters or racehorses for example) profit from being turned loose in a paddock or from being led out for a half hour to pick at grass. 'Sunday off' is convenient for human labour but does nothing for a horse.

The healthiest horses are those which are kept on the move for several hours each day. The happiest are those which go on different, stimulating rides. Bear in mind the wandering habit of a wild horse, and then consider the limitations of a paddock, or, worse, a stable.

Stabled horses need a good grooming every day to promote circulation and to remove irritating loose hairs (horses at grass solve these problems by rolling). Grooming, however, removes protective dust from the coat, and so rugs will be needed to keep the horse warm in cold weather. These rugs can slip, so check the horse frequently.

Never leave a horse in a stable with its coat sweaty from exercise or damp from rain. Restricted movement inhibits circulation, and the horse chills. A

quick way of drying off the body is to heap straw
along the back and cover with a rug (inverted to keep
the lining dry), while rubbing the legs dry with straw.
Remove wet mud: it hardens later and tears the
horse's skin when it is brushed away. It is easier to
wipe off sweat marks at this stage with a damp sponge
and so avoid the coat setting into waves. Clean out
the feet to make sure that the horse has not picked
up stones; also check the shoes for wear.

Good beds for a horse on a hard stable floor are
wheat straw, wood shavings, peat or shredded paper.
Warmth comes from the bedding, so it should be at
least 15cm/6in deep in the middle and piled up to
60cm/2ft or more at the sides to restrict any draughts
and to allow the horse to pull in more bed as he

wishes. Remove wet and dirty bedding daily and top up with fresh.

Food varies with the size of the animal and with the type of work required from it. When the slightest doubt exists ask your veterinarian. In principal, it is natural for horses to pick at food for most of their waking hours, so give three or four small meals a day rather than one main meal at night. Horse nuts are popular but are boring all by themselves, day in and day out. Add appetisers such as carrots and apples and vary the diet with a bran mash a couple of times a week to clean the horse's insides out. Good quality hay – poor hay is dusty and will make the animal cough – should be provided round the clock unless the horse is fat and greedy. Damp hay keeps the dust down. Plentiful fresh water is essential.

Horses kept at grass need daily visiting, even in summertime, to check for condition and injuries. Lift up and inspect the feet on each visit to see that shoes or hooves are not unduly worn and that stones are not lodged in the feet. 'A horse is only as good as its feet' is an old saw, but it is true. Much trouble can be avoided by regular inspection.

Check the water supply. Clean it out when necessary. Check the grazing for poisonous weeds. Check the fencing. Above all, check the horse's physical health to see that he is neither too fat nor too thin and that the bloom on his coat shows well-being. He will indicate his mental health by the degree of his interest in you. If he seems bored or lonely you should take him out more often.

Keeping a horse is time-consuming. Owners who cannot spend at least three hours every day with their animals would be do better to keep their horses in livery stables, where other people will look after them.

Disease

Horses are more delicate than humans. Their furry coats can withstand the rigours of a hard winter, but they can die from a cough or a twisted gut. A horse which coughs more than twice at exercise – especially if it is a dry, hard cough rather than a throat-clearing one – is probably ill. It should not be ridden at faster than a walk until the cause of the cough is known. A horse which rolls a lot, especially if it exhibits patchy sweating when it rolls, is probably suffering from stomach pains. Horses may roll once or twice after exercise but it does not make them sweat. However, a horse with colic will often roll repeatedly in an attempt to straighten out its gut and it sweats from the pain. A veterinary surgeon should be sent for at once. In a case of suspected colic keep the horse moving until the veterinarian arrives.

In a case of 'Monday morning sickness' (azoturia) the horse at first stiffens and later becomes rigid. Call the vet at the first sign.

Listlessness, a running nose, dull eyes or a staring coat are all signs of illness. So is heat – the good horseman constantly checks for a leg which feels hotter than its fellows – and scratches and lumps and sores. Daily inspection is the best guide to a horse's health, so that an owner may know at once when a horse feels or looks different from normal.

Any lameness is a potential disaster. Run a hand down the legs and over the feet each day before exercise to check for unaccustomed heat. Do *not* work the horse if any is present.

Grass-fed horses often pick up worms. They should be wormed three times a year unless grazing with cows, the presence of which interrupts the redworm life cycle, destroying the larvae. Stabled horses should also be wormed.

Tetanus is prevalent in many soils. It can be picked up through the smallest scratch. Horses should be innoculated against it and given booster shots for immunity through their lives (and the same goes for their owners too!).

Catching a disease in its early stages and sending promptly for the veterinarian is both humane and, in the long run, economic.

HORSE AND
PONY BREEDS

The Breeds

Although horses were domesticated by man many centuries ago, most of the breeds of horse and pony that you can see today are comparatively modern inventions.

Climate and terrain have played their part in producing different kinds of horse, especially with island races or others which have developed in remote areas, but most of today's breeds have been produced by man to provide the animal best suited to particular tasks. At one time breeding would have been simply a matter of picking healthy and hard-working animals, but it has become increasingly sophisticated as requirements have become more precise. However, you will find that most breeds are descended from very mixed stock – if you look back far enough into a pedigree you will generally discover ambiguous breeding such as 'by Farmer Smith's bay out of the Squire's good mare'.

Today there is a wide range of horse and pony breeds and new ones are still being created. Differences are sometimes so slight that even the expert could not tell them apart and the layman would see no difference at all. This book presents the world's well-established breeds, omitting some that are so like another that it is debatable whether they can really be considered distinct types.

AKHAL-TEKE

One of the oldest breeds, the Akhal-Teké originates
in the USSR and is the most distinctive strain of the
ancient race of horses known as Turkoman, or
Turkmene. Horses of this type can be traced back to
500BC.

It is a small horse (14.2-15.2 hands high) with a
spare frame and a sparse mane and tail. Its colour is
grey, bay or gold, usually with a metallic bloom to
the coat. It is bold and willful, and can be obstinate
and snappy if displeased. Bred in the deserts of
central Asia, it is supremely resilient and has been
known to travel hundreds of miles without water. It
has magnificent action, with a flowing, elastic stride
at all paces.

ALBINO

Any horse or pony with complete absence of pigmentation is an Albino. It has pink skin, a snow-white coat and pale blue or dark brown eyes.

Albinos usually occur at random but in the United States they have been developed as a breed. **North American Albinos** are handsome, lightweight horses with kindly, intelligent characters. They have been bred since early in this century and are thought to descend from a quality saddle horse named Old King, who may have been an Arab-Morgan cross. Americans aim, with some success, to breed out the weak eyes and the over-sensitivity of the skin to the sun.

ALTER-REAL

This famous Portuguese breed stems from 300 splendid Andalusian mares who were bought by the House of Braganza in 1747 to found a Portuguese National Stud. The breed was decimated by Napoleon and was disastrously outcrossed to foreign breeds, but thoughtful management by the Ministry of Economy in 1932, which bred only from the best Altérs, founded the great quality of the modern breed.

The horse stands 15-16 hands high and is usually bay or brown, though occasionally grey. It is intelligent and highly strung. Given a sympathetic trainer, it makes an outstanding saddle horse.

AMERICAN QUARTER HORSE

This is the most popular breed in the world. It is a gentle horse with a pleasing disposition and in colour is usually chestnut, bay or brown with little or no white on its face and legs. It stands 14.3-16.1 hands high and the official standard of the American Quarter Horse Association describes its general appearance as 'proportionally well built ... symmetrical and smooth with a blending of all component parts, which results in overall balance, style and beauty'.

It is a horse of powerful physique, with a muscular body, massive hindquarters and with fine legs that are slimmer than would be expected to support so strong a body. Its head is short and alert and full of quality, with large wideset eyes and flaring nostrils. In sum, the build is compact and strong with refined extremities.

The Quarter Horse's beginnings lie in the requirements of rich plantation owners in Virginia and the Carolinas. Arab, Barb and Turkish stock, brought in by the Spanish, was crossed in the early seventeenth century with imported English horses to produce a tractable, stylish mount. It was selectively bred for the popular sport of sprint racing which usually took place in the village street and was run over distances up to a quarter of a mile (400m): hence the name Quarter Horse.

It is the oldest of the American breeds. Nowadays more than 1,500,000 Quarter Horses are registered in

America alone and more than 40 nations own these horses. The American Quarter Horse Association in Amarillo, Texas, has to employ over 200 people to handle the largest equine registry in the world.

Quarter Horse racing is popular in Australia as well as in America. However, the top prize is still the All-American Futurity Stakes, run annually in California and worth over half a million dollars to the winner.

This versatile breed is clever with cattle, and in the USA and Canada is still the ablest in rodeo contests. Pioneer ranchers acclaimed it as the most dexterous and intelligent cow horse. It can spin on a dime and jump from a stop to a gallop, and in other respects, as fans all over the world will attest, is also a rewarding mount.

AMERICAN SADDLEBRED
or KENTUCKY SADDLER

Even at the walk, trot and canter – and the Saddlebred has two finer gaits, exclusive to its breed – these horses have the grace of ballet dancers. They were first of all bred largely in Kentucky, as the most fluid-moving and handsome horses that the rich plantation owners of the time (early and middle nineteenth century) could produce. The name Kentucky Saddler still pertains in parts of the United States but the worldwide label of American Saddlebred stems from 1891, when a group of leading dealers founded the American Saddle Horse Breeders' Association in Louisville, Kentucky.

The Saddlebred's exclusive gaits are the slow gait and the rack, and both are designed to give the rider the smoothest of transport. The rack is an even, four-beat movement in which each foot pauses in mid-air, producing a spectacular prance at a gallop speed of up to 30mph (48kph). The slow gait is a slower, more graceful version of the rack, a high-stepping movement. The Saddlebred's walk is flat-footed and springy, its trot high-actioned and its canter smooth and rhythmic.

The Saddlebred came about from a mixture of Thoroughbred and Morgan blood with that of the old, and now extinct, Narragansett Pacer, a high-stepping harness and riding horse with a fluid stride. It was bred to provide rich men with a luxurious, showy ride.

Modern Saddlebreds are usually aimed at the show ring, where they compete in separate classes for three-gaited (walk, trot and canter only) and five-gaited horses according to their prowess.

As would be expected, the Saddlebred is a superb riding horse, adding a charming nature and great presence to its comfortable and spectacular movements. It stands 15-16 hands high and is solid-coloured – bay, black, chestnut and grey are the most common, but it is occasionally roan or palomino, usually with white markings on the face and lower legs. It has a small, alert head with prick ears, gaily carried on an arched neck, a short, muscular body and slim, hard legs. Its extravagant movements are set off by its unnaturally-high tail carriage, which is created by nicking the tail muscles when the horse is young and resetting them in a crupper.

AMERICAN SHETLAND

This slightly taller (up to 11.2 hands high) version of the Scottish island breed is also lighter in build than its ancestor. Its head is more refined, with a faint inward dish and dainty ears. Refinement notwithstanding, it can pull twice its own weight.

Selective beeding from quality imported Shetlands has given it a high action befitting a tiny Hackney. It appears in the show ring in a variety of guises, sometimes with its tail nicked to give artificially high

carriage, sometimes with false tail hair and sometimes even with false hooves to make its feet look longer. It is popular in Pulling Contests, where ponies compete to pull a percentage of their weight, and on the racetrack, where Shetlands have clocked 1 minute 55 seconds on a half-mile (80.5m) track.

AMERICAN STANDARDBRED

The most famous of all modern trotting horses, this is the type most commonly seen harnessed to a buggy on a racetrack. It looks a bit like a small, muscular Thoroughbred, though more of the heavier-set steeplechase type than that of the fierier, more delicate-framed flat racehorse. It tends to be longer

in the body and shorter in the leg than the Thoroughbred and it is usually of a 'commoner' appearance.

Powerfully built with iron legs, the Standardbred is prized for its trotting speed rather than for its pretty looks. It is a small horse, standing only 14-16 hands high. Its body is muscular, with a well-developed chest, and its action at a trot is long-striding and free. The Standardbred's main fault lies in getting its legs out of its own fast-moving way, and in this the wider-chested and longer-bodied horses come off best because it is easier for them to avoid knocking their knees together or slicing their hind feet into their own front shins.

Colours are mostly bay, brown, chestnut or black, sometimes with a bit of white on the face or feet.

The name 'Standardbred' comes from the one-mile (1.6 km) standard speed trial required for race qualification. It applies to both trotters and pacers. Trotters must achieve 2 min 30 sec per standard mile, while pacers must cover the same distance five seconds faster. Pacing, an unnatural gait for a horse, although sometimes it is handed on from mare to foal, is a trot in which both legs on the same side move simultaneously.

Standardbreds are largely of Thoroughbred descent, from which they get their speed, but there is also a mix of Arab, Barb and Morgan, for stamina, and Canadian and Hackney trotting blood for style.

ANDALUSIAN

The great white horse of Spain, famous in modern times through its public feats for the Spanish Riding School of Vienna, is thought originally to have come from Africa. The first recorded import of horses into Spain was of the 2000 Numidean mares brought by Hasdrubal of Carthage, which were left to run wild until the Roman invasion of 200BC and which were claimed to be 'faster than the wind'.

This superb riding horse has strength, elegance and intelligence. It is a proud horse with magnificent bearing, standing around 16 hands high and nearly always grey in coat (though it can be black).

Today's true type of riding horse initially emerged soon after the Vandals, a Teutonic race of barbarians, conquered the part of Spain which was later to be

named Vandalusia in their honour. The Vandals brought along tall, stout-bodied, Germanic horses with slender necks which interbred with the native Spanish stock. The Moslems, who invaded Spain in 711 and stayed for eight centuries, brought 300,000 of the swift and sturdy Barbs. Victories by the agile-mounted Moslems over the Spanish on their heavy German/Spanish horses taught the Spaniards to breed for alertness and manoevrability.

The first official stud, at Cordoba, was started by a Moslem. However, from the time of the conquest of Granada in the eleventh century, the Spanish kings, realising the importance of light cavalry, began to use the horse as a fighting animal. The 'airs above the ground' demonstrated by the Spanish Riding School today are war movements, not circus tricks, and it takes about seven years to train a horse to be proficient in them. The *capriole*, for example, in which the horse leaps vertically into the air from a standstill and kicks out with its hind feet, enabled a hemmed-in warrior to use his horse's hooves as a fighting machine to kick his way free.

Andalusians were nearly wiped out during the reign of King Philip III, due to interbreeding with heavier stallions, and later Napoleon's marshals took the best of the horses home with them. Carthusian monks, fanatically obsessed with purity of line, were the greatest preservers of the Andalusian. Were it not for a few Andulasians concealed by the monks and a small herd hidden by the Zapata family the line of great white horses might have died out. As it was, a new stud was begun in the nineteenth century by King Ferdinand VII's advisers and the Andalusian has prospered ever since.

ANGLO-ARAB

Half English Thoroughbred, half Arab (hence the name), this is a gay, sweet-natured horse. Its quality varies with its breeding; but in general it is an elegant, lightweight saddle horse, standing close to 16 hands high, in colour usually bay or chestnut. It has a healthy, pleasing body and large, expressive eyes.

Anglo-Arabs are bred in several countries, but are most popular in Poland, France and England.

APPALOOSA

A curiously-coloured horse from the United States, the Appaloosa stands 14.2-15.2 hands high and may have any of six basic patterns of spots on a roan background. Skin around the nose, lips and genitalia tends to be mottled, with white eyeballs. Sometimes the hooves are vertically striped.

This is a tractable, durable horse that is handy and quick on its feet. It has a compact body with a short back and its wispy mane and tail are sometimes called 'rat-tailed' or 'finger-tailed'.

Its name is a corruption of that of the Palouse river, which runs through the states of Washington, Idaho

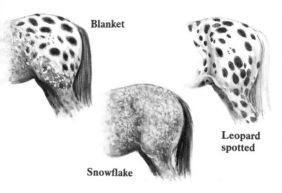

Blanket

Leopard spotted

Snowflake

and Oregon. Its development is attributed to the Nez Percé Indians, who, despite being nearly wiped out in a six-day battle with the US Army, survived to get this breed registered 61 years later. Though still most common in the western United States, the Appaloosa has become so popular that it is now numerically one of the half-dozen top breeds in America.

Its origins are obscure. Horses with similar distinctive colouring appear in ancient Chinese and Persian art and in much earlier cave paintings at Pêche Merle, in France. Probably, like all foundation American horses, it arrived with the Spaniards. But where from? Horses and ponies with Appaloosa colouring exist all over the world, most bearing scant resemblance to the quality Quarter Horse type of the American breed.

ARAB

Allah said to the South Wind, 'Become solid flesh, for I will make a new creature of thee, to the Honour of My Holy Name, and the abasement of Mine enemies, and for a servant to them that are subject to Me.'

The South Wind said, 'Lord, do Thou so.'

Then Allah took a handful of the South Wind and He breathed thereon, creating the horse and saying, 'Thy name shall be Arabian, and virtue bound into the hair of thy forelock, and plunder on thy back. I have preferred thee above all beasts of burden, inasmuch as I have made thy master thy friend. I have given thee the power of flight without wings, be it in onslaught or in retreat. I will set men on thy back, that shall honour and praise Me and sing Hallelujah to My Name.'

This Bedouin legend expresses the near-mystical belief of the desert tribesman in the power of his horse. The exceptional quality of the Arab horse and his purity of line (pure-bred horses are called *asil*, meaning pure, by Arab tribesmen) came about because of the faith of Mohammed, who was convinced of the military importance of good horses for his followers. The text of the Koran, which Mohammed wrote down, includes injunctions to encourage fine breeding and fine feeding of horses.

'So many grains of barley as thou givest thy horse, so many sins shall be forgiven thee,' says the Koran. Also, 'The Evil One dares not enter a tent in which a pure-bred horse is kept.'

Religious commandment, backed by extraordinary natural passion for their horses, led the Bedouin into a man-to-horse relationship unequalled to this day. These fierce desert people shared their food with their horses and even slept with them. Food was scarce in the extremes of heat and cold of the barren Arabian deserts, and because of this the hardy desert horses learned to live on food ranging from dried dates to locusts, from camels' milk to meat.

The mares, not the stallions, were the most highly prized, and were the mounts favoured for war and plunder. Purity of line was regarded with fanatical seriousness and horses were inbred to reinforce their good qualities – a strange idea to western breeders, who think that breeding father to daughter brings out weakness.

Nonetheless, the Arab horse, a small, tough horse (14.2-15.1 hands high) of remarkable spirit, endurance and beauty, has become a founding parent of most of the quality saddle stock of the West.

Arab horses seem first to have been introduced into Europe during the Moorish invasions of the western Mediterranean. Initially, they appear to have been regarded only as decorative parade horses, but their qualities of speed, dexterity and endurance slowly became as much appreciated in northern climes as they already were by the followers of Mohammed.

After the disastrous retreat of the French Army from Moscow in the bitter winter of 1812, Napoleon's aide-de-camp wrote to his superior officer, 'The Arab

horse withstood the exertions and privations better than the European horse. After the cruel campaign in Russia almost all the horses the Emperor had left were his Arabs. General Hubert ... was only able to bring back to France one horse out of his five, and that was an Arab. Captain Simmoneau, of the General Staff, had only his Arab left at the end, and so it was with me also.'

During the Crimean War the Arab stallion Omar Pasha galloped the 93 miles from Silistra to Varna in one day. His rider subsequently died of exhaustion, but the horse was as fresh as ever.

In the early days of the Thoroughbred racehorse Thoroughbreds were matched against Arab horses. The longer-legged Thoroughbred gained supremacy in the first mile or two but, in the end, was exhausted

and defeated. Sturdy Bedouin riders laughed at the puny English jockeys and scoffed at mounts which were not fit to carry on after only three hours of racing.

Today's Arab horse is widely prized in most of Europe and North America. For the most part the pure desert horse has degenerated, in temperate climates, into a softer, fatter animal.

Of the several hundred family lines of the original Bedouin horse, three main types are the ones most seen today. They are:

Kehylan, a masculine type symbolizing power and endurance.

Seglawi, with feminine beauty and elegance.

Muniqi, a spare and angular horse which symbolizes speed.

ARDENNAIS

This massive, compact horse displays the best points of a carthorse and has remained one of the most popular breeds of modern times. It is strong, but so gentle that little children can handle it, even though small enough to walk under its belly.

It comes from the French and Belgian regions of the Ardennes, stands about 15.3 hands high and is bay, roan or chestnut. It is thought to be the horse praised by Julius Caesar in *De Bello Gallico*, and seems likely to have been a Great Horse of the middle ages. It was certainly used by Napoleon to haul his artillery. In modern times it has been of great use to agriculture in the area of its origin.

AUSTRALIAN PONY

This pony is a classic example of selective breeding by man for a specific purpose – in this case to produce a perfect children's riding animal – and a very nice pony it is. Though bred from assorted stock imported into Australia since the early 19th century, its most visible debt is to its Welsh Mountain Pony ancestors.

It is taller than the Welsh Mountain, standing 12-14 hands high, but in other respects the resemblance is very marked. It has the quality head and expressive eyes of the Welsh, along with that breed's gay carriage and smooth, flowing action.

It has been purebred since 1929, when the Australian Pony Stud Book Society was formed.

AUXOIS

This particularly powerful draught horse is a larger version of the Ardennais, which it closely resembles. It comes from the same north-eastern region of France, and from very similar ancestry.

It is a quiet, kind, willing horse, exhibiting a general air of kindliness. It has a large head, set on a short, strong neck, a massive front, a powerful, deep-girthed body and strong hindquarters with a low-set tail. Its legs are short and very sturdy.

Though still occasionally used for agriculture, it is, like many other Continental heavy horses, mainly bred for meat. *Not illustrated.*

AVELIGNESE

The Avelignese is indigenous to Italy. It is a strong and hardy mountain pony, thriving both on snowy heights and under the hot summer sun. Its colour is chestnut, often with a flaxen mane and tail, and it looks much like the Austrian Haflinger, with whom it shares a common ancestry, except that it is a little taller and heavier. It stands 13.3-14.3 hands high.

Avelignese ponies are kindly and placid in temperament. Being, furthermore, sure-footed and seldom subject to illness, they make ideal mountain pack ponies or farm workers. Much of their work today involves carrying tourists on treks, for which they are ideally suited because of their equable, reliable natures.

The Avelignese is said to contain Arab blood, but its looks and docile personality do not lend much substance to this claim.

BALEARIC PONY

Found mostly in Majorca, the largest of the Balearic Islands, this ancient Mediterranean type still looks like the horses shown on Greek coins. Its head is fine and often Roman-nosed, set on a short neck with an upright mane. It is lean and light of bone, though its legs and feet are hard. There is no fixed size, although it is usually under 14 hands high.

It is not an enlivening horse to ride but its gentle, patient nature makes it of great use to small farmers and tradesmen. It is not a prized breed but simply a scrawny pony enduring unfavourable climatic conditions. As such, it looks like other Mediterranean ponies. *Not illustrated.*

BARB

Once the mount of warring tribesmen of north-west Africa, the tough and kindly, though high-mettled Barb is one of the great foundation breeds. For centuries it was used to improve foreign bloodlines. It was taken to Spain in great numbers during the Moorish invasion and, crossed with the taller, less-spirited horses of the Vandals and with the help of other Oriental blood, gave rise to the Andalusian. Later it went to the eastern Mediterranean with

traders from the Barbary Coast. Still later, it went to France and was interbred to produce the Limousin, the French riding horse of the Middle Ages. Even later still, during the reign of racing's great enthusiast King Charles II, it was imported into England to take part in the foundation of the Thoroughbred race-horse.

The famous North African cavalry of recent times, the Spahis, always rode Barb stallions. The Barb is still to be found in Morocco, Tunisia and Algeria, though often the pure line has been infiltrated with Arab blood.

It is a hardy and enduring horse, able to live on little and poor-quality food. Solid in colour, it stands 14-15 hands high and has a long, refined head with wideset eyes, a strong body with long, clean legs and a charismatic bearing. Pure Barb horses are most often seen today performing in displays given by North African tribesmen and cavalry.

BASHKIR

A strong working pony, close to 14 hands high, which has been developed over many centuries in the foothills of the Ural Mountains as an ideal Russian farm animal. It is exceptionally hardy, living out in deep snow in biting temperatures. It is sturdy and strongly built and has abundant mane and tail. Colours are usually bay, chestnut or dun.

Bashkirs pull carts and sleighs, till fields, are ridden and are used as pack animals. They have great powers of endurance. In general it is the males who are worked while the females are kept for milking. *Not illustrated.*

BASUTO

Despite its name, the Basuto pony is not native to Basutoland, though it has been bred there for many decades. It derives from Arabs, Barbs and Thoroughbreds imported by early European settlers into Cape Province. These crosses gave rise to the Cape Horse, which was taken to Basutoland some 150 years ago and deteriorated in size through lack of care and the demands of the arid climate. It has become one of the toughest and bravest ponies in the world.

BAVARIAN WARMBLOOD

This heavy, chestnut warmblood is a modern variation on an old type. Its forerunner is the esteemed old German war horse, the Rottaler, which was bred in the fertile valley of Rott in Lower Bavaria and became famous as a battle charger and later as a draught horse.

The breed has been lightened during the past two centuries by crossing with Norman, Thoroughbred, Cleveland Bay and Oldenburger blood, resulting in a powerful carriage/work horse with a willing nature. The name Rottaler was dropped about 1960 in favour of Bavarian Warmblood. *Not illustrated*.

BEBERBECK

A quality saddle horse, looking like the Thorough-bred, though up to more weight, this horse stands more than 16 hands high and is usually bay or chestnut. It has enough gentle patience to make a good farm or harness horse and enough courage and class to make it useful to the cavalry. Unfortunately only small numbers now survive.

Beberbeck Stud, near Kassel, was founded in 1720. At first it aimed to breed Palominos, but this changed to the breeding of fine saddle and carriage horses. Local mares were bred to Arab stallions and to Thoroughbreds, with quality results. The Stud closed in 1930. Beberbecks are still bred but are no longer an important breed. *Not illustrated*.

BOSNIAN

The Bosnian, an affectionate and intelligent pony, deserves its popularity as the most-loved pony of the Balkan states. It is sturdy and hardy and it has great powers of endurance.

It is a compact mountain pony of the Tarpan type, not unlike the Huçul to look at.

Nearly half a million of these ponies work in Yugoslavia as farm and pack ponies and, in recognition of their usefulness, the State carefully controls their breeding. All stallions used at stud have first to prove themselves by carrying a load of some 100kg/220lb for 16km/10 miles. The best can do it in 1¼ hours.

BOULONNAIS

This most elegant of the French heavy draught horses owes its fine head, with bright eyes and short, pricked ears, to Arab blood. Its strength and size (15.3-16.3 hands high) come from the old Great Horses of northern Europe which carried knights into battle.

It has a grace and harmony unusual for its bulk, enhanced by a silky grey coat and bushy mane. Since its decline as a war horse it has served French agriculture long and well.

Today it is bred for size, because of its value as meat.

BRABANT

The Brabant, or **Belgian Heavy Draught Horse**, is usually red roan with black points, though it can also be bay, brown, dun, grey or chestnut. It stands up to 17 hands high. Its temperament is bold, energetic and good natured. The head is smallish, plain and square, but with an intelligent expression, and the body is immensely strong. The whole animal moves well and has great presence.

This is an outstanding heavy horse. Like its fine compatriot, the Ardennais, it can count Flanders Horses in its distinguished ancestry and is one of the renowned Belgian breeds which have done much to improve foreign coldbloods. Inbreeding for exceptional quality was practised over centuries and, as a result, the Brabant invariably breeds true.

BRETON

The Breton, as its name implies, stems from Brittany.
It is a lively, sweet-tempered heavy horse, usually red
roan in colour but sometimes blue roan, bay, chestnut
or grey. As heavy horses go it is not very tall, standing
14.3-16 hands high, but it compensates by being
compact and muscular.

Two types exist today. The taller and heavier – the
type most widely seen – is the **Breton Heavy
Draught**, a horse which has remarkably little feather
on its legs for so strongly-built a coldblood (*illustrated*). The **Postier Breton**, smaller and more active,
is a medium-weight coach/draught animal with
excellent paces.

BRUMBY

'Brumby' is the name given by Australians to the wild horse of that continent. It is a degenerative scrub horse of high intelligence and is consequently very hard to catch, and, once caught, near-impossible to train.

It has an interesting history. During the great Australian gold rush, in the middle of the nineteenth century, many domestic horses were loosed to run wild in the outback. They bred indiscriminately and, in man's eyes, deteriorated in quality. However, as happens when domestic animals run wild, the brainiest and most adaptable survived. The Australian climate suits the horse and these herds of sharp

'scrubbers' multiplied so rapidly that they soon became agricultural pests. Their numbers were increased when other unwanted horses were freed because of twentieth-century mechanisation.

Culling became necessary if · farmers were to survive. In the early 1960s vast numbers of Brumbies were shot down. Few remain.

BUDYONNY

This superb Russian saddle horse is named for Marshal Budyonny, a famous Revolutionary cavalry leader who founded the breed at the army stud at Rostov early in the twentieth century.

The main bloodline is Thoroughbred-Don, with infusions of Kazakh and Kirgiz. The best youngsters,

selected for their cavalry potential, were carefully reared and were subjected to mental and physical aptitude tests. Thus this all-round riding horse got away to a selective start. By 1948 it had become sufficiently recognizable to be fixed as a breed.

Now that cavalry is redundant, the Budyonny excels at taxing tests such as eventing. It stands 15.2-16 hands high and its chestnut or bay coat often shows the typical metallic sheen of the best Russian saddle breeds.

BURMA PONY

Also known as the **Shan**, this unimpressive-looking pony, standing around 13 hands high, is bred mainly by the hill people of East Burma (Shan States). Although strong and active as a working pony, horseless British officers stationed in Burma found it mentally and physically sluggish as a polo pony. It lacks the élan of temperate-climate ponies. *Not illustrated*.

CAMARGUAIS

The famous white horse of the Camargue is in fact a pony, standing around 14 hands high. It has lived wild in the watery Rhône delta in southern France from beyond memory.

The Camarguais is a primitive breed of great antiquity. It looks arguably like the 17,000-year-old cave paintings of Lascaux, though there are also

indications of more recent oriental blood in its expressive head and short, wideset ears.

In recent centuries it has been the traditional mount of the *gardiens*, the cowboys of Provence, and is still used for this purpose. Otherwise it continues to live wild, except for increasing use by tourist riders in its beautiful but treacherous habitat.

A Romany legend, dating back to time out of mind, concerns the Camargue horses. The arrival of Sarah, their patron saint, is still enacted each year on the Mediterranean shore.

Sarah is supposed to have come from Egypt by boat. When she landed she dressed her long auburn hair, and the olive pollen released by her comb

scattered on the wind and brought the first olive trees to France. Her annual re-arrival is celebrated by carrying her statue out to sea and then returning her in triumph to the church, accompanied by an escort of gypsies and mounted *gardiens*.

The festival of *Les Saintes Maries*, as this is called, is one of rejoicing. Precious stones and flowers are laid at Sarah's feet.

Saintes Maries takes place in May, when the Romany life comes into its easiest period. In winter, when forage for horses and man is scarce, the Romany's time is harder than that for most other men and the white horses of the Camargue find little to eat in their watery homeland.

CANADIAN CUTTING HORSE

This horse is very similar to the American Quarter Horse, from which it is almost exclusively descended. Emphasis has been placed on its use as a cow pony rather than on its speed as a short-distance racehorse, resulting in slight physical variations.

Long-bodied, strong-legged and highly intelligent, it can carry a cowboy all day and seems to have an innate talent for cutting a cow away from the rest of the herd. It stands around 15.2-16.1 hands high and its colour can be any solid colour, though chestnut predominates.

The Canadian Cutting Horse turns unusually quickly on the foot because of the immense strength of its hindquarters and can jump from a standstill to a gallop with remarkable speed.

In pre-machine days, this horse had immense value to Canadian cattle farmers. In present times ground vehicles and airplanes have largely replaced it in terms of necessary work. Now it has a different way of earning its keep: far from working the home herd, it is used to win substantial prizes in cattle-cutting competitions.

CASPIAN

A little pony (10-12 hands high) coloured chestnut, bay, brown or grey. With its fine bone and short back, this is more like a miniature horse than a pony. Its head is Arab-like, with small, pricked ears and large eyes. Its mane and tail are silky and fine.

The Caspian is quick on its feet, with remarkable balance. It jumps like a cat.

Today's Persian pony is believed to be the tiny wild horse of Mesopotamia, which was used for ceremonial purposes nearly 5000 years ago. It was thought, for many centuries, to be extinct, but in the spring of 1965 a few ponies of Caspian type were noticed pulling carts on the shoreline of the Caspian Sea.

The ponies were removed to the safety of the Nourouzabad Stud in Teheran to be carefully studied. Bone and blood comparisons suggest that these ponies are very like the ancient miniature horses of Mesopotamia.

Caspian ponies are tough and hardy, with great qualities of endurance. Now mostly relieved from their farming duties, they are used as children's riding ponies and for racing in Iran.

CHAROLLAIS HALFBRED

A strongly-built French saddle horse with a kind and intelligent disposition, which is bred of quality stock, half Thoroughbred and half Anglo-Norman. It was originally bred as a cavalry horse. This function having now become obsolete, it is presently popular as a hunter.

It stands 15-16 hands high and is so similar in type to the closely-related Bourbonnais and Nivernais Halfbreds of neighbouring regions that all three horses are usually collectively called **Demi-Sang Charollais**. *Not illustrated.*

CHINCOTEAGUE and ASSATEAGUE

These two ponies, named for two small islands off the temperate coast of the south-eastern United States, are virtually indistinguishable. Pinto is their commonest colour, but there is no colour rule.

Though they stand only 12 hands high their build is that of a small horse rather than of a pony. Photographs that do not indicate scale suggest that they are inferior lightweight horses.

They are stubborn and intractable, though occasionally making good riding ponies.

No one can account for their surprising presence on their islands. It is guessed that they may have swum from a ship wrecked on the Virginia coast.

CLEVELAND BAY

The Cleveland Bay may well be the oldest carriage horse breed of the British Isles. It is certainly the most enduring. Thanks to the interest of Queen Elizabeth II, who began breeding from the few descendants of this horse in the 1960s, the Cleveland Bay has been regenerated. Though tall and unwieldy for modern carriage-driving competitions, royally-owned teams of Cleveland Bays have helped to win Prince Philip world-class eminence as a coachman.

It stands 16-16.2 hands high, though the Cleveland Bay Horse Society will not disqualify good animals outside this size. It must be bay with black points (legs, mane and tail). Grey hairs in the mane or tail,

far from disqualifying the horse, are recognized as signifying pure Cleveland blood.

The Cleveland Bay stems from the Chapman Horse which was used by chapmen (travelling merchants) in medieval times. It originates from Yorkshire. Given a dash of Thoroughbred blood, which made it taller and more refined, it has become the coaching aristocrat of modern times.

CLYDESDALE

One of the four existing breeds of British heavy horse and the only one surviving in Scotland, the Clydesdale is easily distinguishable by abundant white on its face and by white feather running up the insides of

its legs and often appearing on its underbelly. The rest of its coat is usually red roan, bay, brown or black.

Like most British heavy horses, Clydesdales stem from Flemish stock imported early in the eighteenth century for pack and agricultural work. However, the singlemindedness of purpose with which Clydesdales were bred is due to the development, shortly after the Flemish horses arrived in Scotland, of the coalfields of Lanarkshire (Clydesdale is the ancient name of Lanarkshire).

The discovery of rich seams of coal quickly lead to vast improvements in the roads leading to the mines. Wheeled vehicles could be pulled along these new roads and sure-footed pack horses, able to carry only limited loads on their backs, began to give way to bigger, bulkier animals who could haul very much greater weights in harness than any horse could carry on its back. Mine owners speedily bred their strongest mares to the massive Flemish stallions. The result became known as the Clydesdale.

This tractable, active horse has since been of great service to Scotland as a farm horse and as a timber-pulling horse. He has also been a valuable export, becoming popular in Australia, New Zealand, the United States (American Clydesdale Horse Association founded 1878), Canada, Russia and Germany.

This kindly giant of horseflesh still has human lovers, but today is bred less for the plough and more to stand, beribboned, at a horse show.

COMTOIS

A small, stocky draught horse of the Franco-Swiss mountain borders, the Comtois is bold, sure-footed and hardy. It stands 14.3-15.3 hands high and is usually bay, though chestnut coats are often seen, with a tendency to lighter manes and tails. It looks not unlike a Postier Breton.

This strong-bodied little horse stands up to extremes of weather. It draws a sleigh at a winter sports resort just as readily as it drags a log from a humid summer forest. *Not illustrated*.

CONNEMARA

This most popular of Irish ponies is an ancient breed and is probably of the same parentage as the Highland

pony of the Western Isles of Scotland. It is named for the westernmost county of Ireland, where it has run wild in the mountains and bogs from times before man thought to record it. It probably originated from horses which swam ashore from wrecks of the Spanish Armada and which, over the centuries, scaled down to suit its colder environment. 'Improvements' by man, using Welsh and Thoroughbred blood, later helped to shape it.

Modern Connemaras stand 13-14.2 hands high and are among the finest and most sure-footed riding ponies in the world.

This is a pony which can easily adapt to horse stature when richly nourished. It has contributed substantially to show jumping and eventing progeny. Typical Connemara ponies retain their characteristics best on poor keep.

CRIOLLO

One of the toughest and soundest breeds in the world, the little Argentinian Criollo (14-15 hands high) is the famous gaucho mount of the great central stock plains. Its powerful, muscular body and short, strong legs, combined with its quickness of mind, make it the ideal cattle-cutting pony. It seldom goes lame. Further, it can survive in extremes of climate and on minimal rations.

Classically, it is dun with a donkey-like dorsal stripe of dark brown down its back and faint 'zebra'

stripes on its legs. Other common colours include roan, liver chestnut and palomino, usually with white markings on the face and legs. Chestnut, bay, black and grey are also seen.

As with all South American horses, its basic blood is Spanish. Criollos stem from Andalusian, Barb and Arab horses, bred thousands of miles away and transported across the Atlantic in sailing ships. Running wild for 300 years accounts for its smaller size, while the muted dun coat is guessed to have evolved as natural protection.

The Criollos' worldwide popularity today is due to their natural expertise as polo ponies.

DALES

This large and powerful pony (14-14.2 hands high) from the dales of northern England is jet black, dark bay or dark brown (known locally as heckberry). Small white markings are acceptable in the breed but large white markings suggest an outcross.

It has a sensible and gentle nature and, as a weight-carrier, it has become an ideal pony-trekking mount. It was used 200-300 years ago as a pack pony, to carry lead from the lead mines to the coast. Next it was used as a farm animal, and soon after was interbred with a famous Welsh Cob trotting stallion to give it flair in harness. As a riding animal it was much liked by such passenger horsemen as the local

doctor, but notwithstanding its all-round talents it almost became extinct with the advent of heavy machinery and cars. Its revival is largely due to the present pony-trekking trade.

DANUBIAN

This handsome, compact animal with a neat, expressive head, powerful hindquarters and hard legs (which look deceptively slender, like those of the American Quarter Horse) on its dense and muscular body, conveys an impression of power and vigour without coarseness.

It is a good saddle horse and makes a useful jumper, especially when crossed with Thoroughbred blood; but, surprisingly, it seems mainly to be thought of as a draught horse in its native Bulgaria.

A twentieth-century product of the Bulgarian State Stud near Pleven, developed from Nonius stallions cross-bred with Anglo-Arab mares, it stands about 15.2 hands high. Usually black or dark chestnut, it is seldom seen outside its native land. *Not illustrated.*

DARASHOURI

This little-known breed is a splendid small saddle horse, very similar to the Arab in looks and movement. Its silky coat appears in most solid colours. Averaging 15 hands high, with a lightweight frame, it is at once elegant, hardy and enduring. *Not illustrated.*

DARTMOOR

'There is on Dartmoor a breed of ponies much in request in that vicinity, being sure-footed and hardy, and admirably calculated to scramble over the rough roads and dreary hills of that mountainous district,' wrote William Youatt, a traveller to Dartmoor, in 1820. 'The Dartmoor pony is larger than the Exmoor [*maybe it then was*], and, if possible, uglier. He exists there almost in a state of nature.

'The late Captain Colgrove, governor of the prison, had a great desire to possess one of them of somewhat superior figure to its fellows; and having several men to assist him, they separated it from the herd. They drove it on some rocks by the side of a tor. A man followed on horseback, while the captain stood below watching the chase. The little animal, being driven into a corner, leaped completely over man and horse and escaped.'

Youatt arrived late on the Dartmoor pony scene. From long beyond the memory of man ponies of a small, hardy riding type have run wild on the moorland of southwest England surrounding the River Dart, but until the end of the nineteenth century they varied so much in type that nobody thought to register them as a breed.

The first recorded mention of the Dartmoor pony appeared in 1012, and from the twelfth to the fifteenth centuries it was tamed and made to carry tin from the Cornish mines. Subsequently, when these mines were exhausted, many were again left to run

free (although some were retained for farm work).

By early in the twentieth century there were just three distinct herds left. One was bay with a mealy muzzle, one dark brown with a light-mealy nose and the third was grey. The Leat, a tiny half-Arab stallion, looking to all intents like a native Dartmoor and foaled in 1918, has been the greatest influence on the modern strain.

Dartmoors were hard-hit in World War II, when their terrain was commandeered by the army. Their recovery has been carefully monitored and breed standards are strictly kept to.

Today's Dartmoor is a hardy, nimble pony standing not more than 12.2 hands high. It is good-natured and sensible – and a good jumper. It makes an ideal first pony for a child.

DØLE-GUDBRANDSDAL

Easily the most influential and most widespread breed in Norway, this sturdy small horse is very like the strong Dales pony of northern England (for whose ancestry it is thought to have been partly responsible). There are also overtones of the black Friesian horse of Holland. It is probably pointless to speculate on which came first. Black and near-black middle-sized animals of hardy, near-coldblood type exist on all sides of the North Sea. They probably stem from the prehistoric Forest and Steppe horses and adapted themselves to suit regional requirements.

There are also signs of Thoroughbred blood in the modern Døle-Gudbrandsdal, since this horse has

more vitality than the coldblood breeds. Other outcrosses of breeding have led to a great variety of Døle types, with the result that this extremely hardy horse can work well hauling timber in sub-zero temperatures, will do all kinds of farm work and is also a calm, sure-footed saddle animal.

Average height is 15 hands. Colours are usually black, brown or bay – near black in most instances – and the coat is predictably dense, in accordance with the cold climate in which it lives, with long, thick mane and tail and feather on its heels.

The demand for Døle horses peaked in the Second World War because of petrol rationing. Since then it has declined as a work horse and is mostly used for riding.

DØLE TROTTER

This Norwegian harness horse, standing a little over 15 hands high, is a classic example of the Døle-Gudbrandsdal when refined for a specific use.

The Døle Trotter was evolved from native stock to meet the fashionable requirements of its time when, some century and a half ago, these were for a swift, attractive horse to pull a lightweight cart. So, in 1834, the Thoroughbred stallion Odin was imported from Britain to give an extra edge to the commonplace Døle horse.

Later infusions of trotting blood only added to the abilities of this tough, competitive trotter. *Not illustrated.*

DON

This powerful Russian saddle horse is energetic, capable and calm. Though its conformation is often faulty and its action on the short side, its stamina and hardiness are so splendid that its fame endures through history.

This was the Cossack horse which galloped into the attack, again and again, when Napoleon's horses died of weakness during the weary retreat from Moscow in the bitter winter of 1812. When the French were finally gone – and mostly dead – these Cossack mounts then survived the long haul home to Moscow. Subsequent infusions of oriental-type blood have made it taller and more handsome.

Today's Don still has unusual stamina. It stands around 16 hands high and its solid-coloured coat often has a golden sheen.

DULMEN

The Dulmen pony of Westphalia is the sole survivor of Germany's two native pony breeds (the other, the Senner, ran wild in the forests of the Teutoberger Wald). Few Dulmens are left either: the only existing herd, of 100 or so mares, runs half-wild on a reserve in its native haunt, the Meerfelder Bruch, but it is privately owned.

These ponies are probably not quite purely bred, owing allegiance to Polish and British pony stallions.

Conversely, their bloodlines are thought to have contributed to the Hanoverian horse.

They stand about 12.3 hands high and are usually dun, black or brown.

DUTCH DRAUGHT

Being largely of Belgian blood, this massive carthorse looks very like the Brabant, or Belgian Heavy Draught Horse.

The Dutch Draught is a fairly recent refinement as a breed, records having been kept in official stud books only since 1925. It is a tall horse, standing about 16.3 hands high, and has good conformation: straight face, wideset intelligent eyes, short alert ears, a short powerful neck and a massive front with huge heart room and puny withers. Its girth is deep, with wide-sprung ribs embracing a powerful body; the whole hung close to the ground on short, muscular legs with feet of iron. Its loins and hindquarters are heavily muscled.

It is a quiet horse with a very kind spirit, but it works boldly when required. Its action is easy and straight and it carries itself well.

It stems from the old Zeeland horses, with additions of Brabant, Ardennais and Oriental blood to gee up its personality into a more active type which was more useful on the lighter, man-made soil of Holland.

The usual colours are chestnut, bay or grey. *Not illustrated.*

EAST BULGARIAN

An excellent riding horse, standing close to 16 hands high, it is largely of Thoroughbred stock but has Arab and Anglo-Arab additions. The breed was fixed early in the twentieth century, since when Thoroughbred blood only has been added.

Developed on two state-owned farms in this communist country, this horse is expected to work in agriculture as well as under saddle. It is therefore extremely versatile.

It is rarely possible to produce a horse which has the strength and patience to pull a plough and also the fire and speed to win a race. However, East Bulgarians, which seem to have a natural aptitude for sport, often do well in the famous Grand Pardubice

of Czechoslovakia, a taxing 7250m (4½mile) steeple-chase run largely over ploughed fields with varied jumps.

EAST FRIESIAN

Until the division of Germany, at the end of World War II, the East Friesian and the Oldenburg belonged to the same breed. Since then the horses have been developed separately. The East Friesian, thanks to Arab blood, has become smaller and fierier than its West German counterpart.

It is now a quality saddle horse, similar to the Oldenburg but with a more refined head and a lighter frame. It stands 16-16.2 hands high.

EINSIEDLER (SWISS HALF-BRED)

The best of the Swiss saddle breeds, and very similar in looks to the Anglo-Norman, this is a tall, all-purpose riding horse resulting from careful selection of Thoroughbred stock and the finest of the local mares. Stallions allowed to mate with the Swiss mares are chosen for the proven performance of both themselves and their parents and include horses of mixed European birth. These stallions must also be of good conformation and stand at least 16.2 hands high.

Modern Einsiedlers are quality all-rounders of the halfbred type.

EXMOOR PONY

Exmoors are reckoned the oldest of the British native breeds. There is no remembrance of how they arrived in their moorland habitat in south-west England. Their ancestors are assumed to have walked in before the landmass of the British Isles split away from the European continent.

They stand between 11.2 and 12.3 hands high and are coloured bay, brown or dun. They have wideset, prominent eyes – 'toad' eyes, more slanting and heavy-lidded than those of most other breeds.

A distinctive feature, common to all Exmoors, is the cream-coloured, 'mealy' muzzle, which looks as though the pony had dropped its mouth into a sack of flour. Their coats are of a peculiar nature, being hard and springy. In summer the coat lies close to the body and shines like brass, but in winter it is long and shaggy and carries no bloom.

Exmoors are hardy little animals, of a wiry dexterity and of great strength for their size. An early nineteenth century writer reports that:

'a well-known sportsman ... rode one of them half-a-dozen miles and never felt such power and action in so small a compass before. To show his accomplishments, he was turned over a gate at least 8 inches higher than his back; and his owner, who rides 14 stone, travelled on him from Bristol to South Moulton, 86 miles, beating the coach which runs the same road.'

Outcrosses of Exmoor with taller horses seldom possess the same hardiness. On the other hand, the brains and cat-like jump are there, and consequently such crosses have produced some splendid hunters, show jumpers and eventers.

FALABELLA

The Falabella is the smallest horse in the world. It comes from Argentina and takes its name from the Falabella family, who developed it on their Recreo de Roca Ranch near Buenos Aires by crossing an extremely small Thoroughbred stallion with the smallest of Shetland mares.

Incredibly, the Falabella stands under seven hands high (72cm/28in tall) and can walk under a dinner table. Its proportions are those of a miniature horse rather than of a pony. Any colour is acceptable in this midget breed, although Appaloosa markings are preferred.

Though friendly and intelligent, the Falabella has scant practical use other than as a pet.

FELL

Coming from the northernmost counties of England – from the steep hillsides of Westmorland and Cumberland – the robust but gentle Fell was once the doctor's favourite mount. It stands 13-14 hands high, and so is slightly smaller than its close relative the Dales pony. In colour it is black, brown or bay, preferably with no white markings.

The Fell is typical of the burly, dark-coated pony breeds seen around all fringes of the North Sea (Dale, Friesian and Døle-Gudbrandsdal), but its shoulder development makes it a more comfortable ride than most of its relatives. Outcrosses with taller Thoroughbred horses produce sure-footed, sensible hunters.

Once used as a hill-farm animal, it is today popular as a trekking pony.

FINNISH

In Finland, horses are traditionally judged by what they can do, regardless of what they look like or who their parents were. The Finnish horse which has evolved through such sensible selection is a fairly large (about 15.2 hands high) all-rounder which combines the sweet nature and stamina of cold-blood breeds with the speed and courage of the warm-bloods.

It is a robust, long-lived horse with a straight action. It trots extremely well. Its thick mane and tail and a touch of feather on its heels protect it against the icy east-European winters. Usually chestnut, it may also be bay, brown or black. It is at once a good farm worker and a nice horse to ride.

FJORD

The Fjord pony of Norway is one of very few breeds which look recognizably the same nowadays as they must have looked beyond the recall of man. It is a strongly-built, primeval sort of pony with a remarkable upright mane. Characteristically, it is coloured dun or cream with a dorsal stripe and stripes on the insides of its forelegs and thighs. The mane and tail are black and silver, with whiter hairs growing on either side of a central dark ridge of mane. It stands 13-14.2 hands high.

It was beloved by the Vikings for horse fights. It is still used in the mountain farms of Norway, where its courage and hardiness exceed the powers of motor vehicles.

FRANCHES MONTAGNES

This horse is a heavy Cob type, averaging 15 hands in height, with a long, low-slung body and short legs with plenty of bone and a bit of feather on the heels. Shoulders and hindquarters show immense power. The neck is short and thick, and the head is comparatively fine with small, pricked ears.

It was developed for local agricultural purposes in the Swiss Jura mountain area, about a century ago. Quality saddle stallions of half-Thoroughbred blood were bred onto stout local mares. Ardennais carthorse blood made up the balance and the result, which suits a mountainous environment, is an active, intelligent horse of great strength.

FREDERIKSBORG

Usually chestnut and standing around 16 hands high, this is a strong and active harness horse, not much different from the carriage-pulling Cleveland Bay in physique.

This Danish breed is a refinement of the medieval horse of the Royal Stud, founded by King Frederick II in 1562 to provide intelligent cavalry horses for the royal stables. These horses became so popular that most were sold abroad. Eventually so few remained in Denmark to breed from that the Royal Stud had to be dissolved in 1839.

The modern Frederiksborg's connection with this breed is tenuous, due to new blood being introduced from outside.

FREIBERGER SADDLE HORSE

A strong, compact riding horse noted for its sure-footedness, this is a taller and lighter version of the Franches-Montagnes of the mountains of western Switzerland, to which it is closely related. Infusions of Arab and Anglo-Norman blood onto the sturdy Frances-Montagnes strain since World War II have produced an excellent saddle temperament – the Freiberger is alert, intelligent, willing and docile – and a physique built for endurance.

The Freiberger stands 15.2-16.1 hands high. Its coat can be any solid colour.

FRENCH SADDLE HORSE

The *Cheval de Selle Français* as it is called in its native land, is a quality halfbred type of horse with speed, stamina and jumping ability. It is a competition horse, used mainly in racing (in special classes for horses which are not pure Thoroughbred) and in show jumping, eventing and cross-country racing.

It is not itself a pure breed; rather, it is a mixture of Thoroughbred, Arab, Anglo-Arab and French Trotter blood with attractive native mares standing, in general, 15-16 hands high. The aim of all this inter-breeding has been, and is, the production of an

elegant-looking riding horse with an active, powerful body. It is the sort of horse which would have been very popular with the cavalry (but unfortunately it does not seem to have been thought of as an end in itself until 1958).

Because of the mixed breeding, which to date produces no absolute standard type, modern French Saddle Horses are not classified until they are three-year-olds and nearly grown up. For show purposes, they are then divided into medium-weights and heavy-weights and also into small (15.3 hands high and under), medium (15.3-16.1 hands high) and large (over 16.1 hands high). All colours are acceptable, though chestnuts and bays are most common.

FRENCH TROTTER

France is the only country to continue the old practice of ridden as well as driven trotting races and, because of this, the French Trotter is a taller (around 16.2 hands high), more powerful type of horse than is usual in international trotting. The French horse must be capable of carrying weights of up to 72.5kg (160lb) over quite long distances.

French Trotters became recognized as a breed in 1922. For more than a hundred years before that English Thoroughbreds, the now-extinct Norfolk Roadsters of trotting fame, and, more latterly, the fast Standardbred trotters of America were imported to interbreed with local mares. The result is a trotting

horse of international speed, but which also has unique stamina.

FRIESIAN

This is one of the oldest breeds, thought to descend from a heavy, coldblood type which lived in Friesland, in the north of Holland, some 3000 years ago. It is also one of the most distinctive-looking, being jet black in colour (white markings are thought most undesirable) with a long face, short prick ears and a slighter depth of girth than its powerful quarters and legs would suggest. It has an exceptional growth of mane and tail, and feather on its heels.

The Friesian has a remarkably pleasant temperament, exciting comments such as 'cheerful',

'loyal' and 'very sensitive'. It is an excellent carriage horse – a winner at World Championship Carriage Driving level – and is a good all-round work horse.

FURIOSO

A strong all-purpose riding horse with an aristocratic head, the Furioso stands about 16 hands high. Founded some 150 years ago in Hungary, this breed has become popular in most Eastern-bloc countries. It excels at show jumping, dressage, eventing and steeplechasing (halfbred horses are often raced in Eastern Europe), and is also an imposing carriage horse.

The breed stems from an English Thoroughbred stallion named Furioso which was bought by the

Hungarian stud farm of Mezöhegyes in 1841 and bred onto local mares of the Nonius type. Other Thoroughbred blood – notably that of North Star in the 1850s – refined the breed further.

GALICENO

A little (12-13.2 hands high) lightly-built animal popular throughout the Americas, the Galiceno originated in Galicia in the north-west of Spain and was introduced, initially to Mexico, by the Conquistadores.

In type it is a small horse rather than a pony, having long legs on a narrow body and a fine head with large eyes. It is hardy, intelligent and docile, and it has a curious, natural running walk.

GARRANO

A very small (10-12 hands high) and pretty pony, dark chestnut in colour and with profuse mane and tail, the Garrano has thrived in the rich mountain pastures of Garrano do Minho and Traz dos Montes in Portugal since time out of mind. Immensely strong, although lightly built, Garranos are used as pack ponies and in agricultural work. *Not illustrated.*

GELDERLANDER

A splendid carriage horse with power, a gay head carriage and a stylish action, this old Dutch breed has

been crossed with the heavier, farm-working Groningen to produce the Dutch Warmblood, a horse of special power and spring of which the late Caroline Bradley's show jumping stallion, Marius, was an outstanding example.

Gelderlanders tend towards a plainish head, but their expression is intelligent. Their bodies are compact and strong, broad and deep, with strong legs, powerful hindquarters and tails set high and held with exaggerated carriage. Their legs are short and strong, with hard, round feet.

They stand 15.2-16 hands high and are usually chestnut or grey. They are tractable and docile, but very active.

GERMAN TROTTER

Smaller than the French Trotter, this is a rather handsome horse with an expressive head. It stands around 15.3 hands high and has a well-developed, robust body with lean, muscular hindquarters, hard, fine legs and a splendid, long-striding action.

In West Germany trotting is twice as popular as Thoroughbred racing and so the breed is kept to an exacting standard by a system of handicapping based on speed over 1000 metres.

Russian Orlov Trotters were the basis of the modern German breed, but it has since been greatly improved by American Standardbred and French Trotter blood.

GOTLAND

The oldest of the Scandinavian pony breeds, this gentle little (12-13.2 hands high) animal has been on the Swedish island of Gotland for longer than man can remember. It is thought to be one of the direct descendants of the Tarpan and shares many characteristics with the Tarpan-like Konik and Huçul ponies.

Despite apparent poorness of bone in its hind legs, it moves well at the walk and at the trot (but gallops badly) and is an excellent jumper.

Oriental blood is thought to have been introduced to the Gotland pony more than a century ago.

GREEK PONIES

Of the tough and scraggy little ponies which endure Greece's summer heat and winter cold, the **Skyros** (*illustrated*) is the smallest. It stands 9.1-11 hands high and lives out wild in the mountains of Skyros, an island to the north-east of Athens, for most of the year. At harvest time it is caught and chased round, three or four tied together, to thresh the corn by trampling. Attempts to breed larger ponies failed, because they could not weather the hard winters.

From the mainland there are also the **Pindos** ponies, 12-13 hands high, bred in the mountains of Thessaly and Epirus since ancient times and used for pack and agriculture and for breeding mules, and the slightly taller, oriental-looking **Peneian** ponies from the Peloponnesos.

GRONINGEN

A tall and sturdy horse from Holland, one of the older breeds, the Groningen stands 15.2-16 hands high or more. It is a kindly friend with a sound constitution and is a frugal horse to keep, working well on paltry food.

It is gentle, obedient, willing and enduring, with a handsome head (despite rather long ears) and a high-set, gaily-carried tail. It works well in harness, having a stylish action, and is a good heavyweight saddle horse. The breed was developed from heavy Friesian horses crossed with East Friesian and Oldenburg blood. Unfortunately, it has now become rare.

HACKNEY

Still much-loved in the show rings of the world, this is the most brilliant of movers. Its crest is gaily arched and its knees snap up smartly almost into its chin. It has a wonderful, rounded, exhilarating stride, as if each separate leg were pinged up out of an elastic band.

It had its heyday almost a century ago, pulling the smartly-painted lightweight carts of the most successful tradesmen: gleaming brass, immaculate leather harness, shining horse with plaited mane on a gaily-held neck, the face held vertical with pricked ears and the docked tail sticking up proudly like a flag in front of the cart's perfect paintwork.

Yet the origin of the name 'hackney' is derogatory. It comes from the Norman French *haquenai*, which in the middle ages was applied to riding animals of the humblest caste.

He wened have repreved be
Of theft or mordre if that he
Had in his stable any Hakenay...

wrote Chaucer. The Old French *haque*, Old Portuguese *faca* and Spanish *haca* all meant 'nag'. 'Hack', in the old sense of hireling, rather than in that of today's show ring riding horse, obviously derives from this.

But what has this to do with the Hackney as we know it? Nothing, except for an influential ancestor a long time ago. Around 1755 a horse called Original

Hackney Horse

Hackney Pony

Shales was foaled by the Thoroughbred Blaze (by Flying Childers by the Darley Arabian, one of the three foundation sires of the Thoroughbred racehorse) out of a mare described as a Hackney. This horse, Original Shales, despite his humble mother, was the father of two regional types of trotting horse: the Yorkshire and the much more famous Norfolk Roadster.

Shales's progeny, the forerunners of the modern Hackney, were initially used chiefly as riding horses. In trotting contests they recorded some formidable feats of speed and endurance, both under saddle and in the shafts as farmers sped to market. Quite quickly, as the golden age of coaching and carriage driving came in with the new tarmacadamed roads, the best of these trotters were recruited for the fanciest *équipages* and the incentive was there to improve the breed with the stamina of Welsh and Fell Pony blood and the speed and class of the Thoroughbred and Arab.

Today's Hackney is divided naturally by size into Hackney Horse classes (in excess of 14.2 hands high) and Hackney Pony classes (under 14.2 hands – and usually more pony-like in conformation). In America, which has taken the Hackney to its heart, the greatest variations in height exist: horses standing up to 16 hands high, and ponies, called 'Bantam' Hackneys, being as little as 11 hands high.

Conventional colours are preferred – bay, brown, black or chestnut – with not much white about them except to pinpoint the flashy movement of the feet.

118

HAFLINGER

A pretty pony from the Austrian Tirol, the Haflinger is almost always chestnut with a thick and flaxen-coloured mane and tail and white markings on the face. Its muzzle is narrow and pointed.

It is tall (about 14 hands high) and sturdy for a pony, and is a marvellous trekking or pack animal. Reared on mountain pastures in extremities of weather and fodder, it is usually left to mature by itself until four years old. This early life without the hammer of man's demands may account for its reputation to live to extraordinary old age – the Haflinger is said to be able to work until it is 40.

HANOVERIAN

Balance, brain and power have combined to make the Hanoverian the most prized dressage and show jumping horse in the modern world. The breed began in the 17th century, in Hanover and Lower Saxony, as a strain of the great Hanoverian Creams, also called the Isabella after the Queen of Spain, which had Andalusian blood. These Creams were bred under British royal patronage at the Landgestüt at Celle in Hanover and were used as carriage horses on state occasions. (The British royal family of the time was Hanoverian by birth).

Recent modification with Thoroughbred and Trakehner blood, while slightly reducing the Hanoverian's power, has made it more elastic in its scope. It has become a tall and powerful riding horse, standing 15.3-17 hands high; yet it is compact and versatile and has excellent balance. In character it is courageous and intelligent. It is well-mannered and strives to do as its rider wishes.

HIGHLAND PONY

Biggest and strongest of all the British pony breeds, the Highland has been known to carry at a canter (in a circus act) seven adult riders weighing collectively some 380kg (840lb) without difficulty.

Until fairly recently there were two types of Highland: the powerful Garron, or Mainland, type with broad back and muscular, crested neck, and the smaller and finer-limbed Western Isles type. Today no official distinction is made between them.

The Highland pony, despite its placid temperament, is responsive and sensitive and can become sour and hard to handle if treated unkindly. It tends

to be wary of strangers, yet will give its trust generously to an owner in whom it has confidence. It can then perform tasks which would be nerve-wracking for most other breeds: as a classic example, the well-treated Highland is the pony which carries the newly-killed stags home from the Scottish shoots.

In the past, the Highland was the Scottish crofter's (smallholder's) pony of all work. Nowadays its sure-footedness makes it popular for trekking, though it is a very versatile animal and is also used variously as a family pony, hunter, hack and in harness.

Shades of dun are its commonest colour, usually with the dark dorsal stripe and zebra markings inside the forelegs which denote the older breeds. Grey, brown, black and liver chestnut are also seen, sometimes with silver-blonde mane and tail.

HISPANO

A Spanish Anglo-Arab from the provinces of Estremadura and Andalusia, this breed is the result of a cross between Spanish Arabian mares and English Thoroughbred stallions. The result is a splendid lightweight saddle horse standing around 16 hands high.

The Hispano is quick on its feet and brave. It excels in sporting competitions and is also used to test the courage of young bulls (the rider pushes the bull over with a pole to see if it will come back fighting; the horse needs to be nimble and quick-thinking). *Not illustrated*.

HOLSTEINER

One of the oldest of the German warmblood breeds, this splendid animal stems from the fourteenth-century Marsh Horse, one of the heavy Great Horse types used for medieval warfare. Spanish (Andalusian), Neapolitan and oriental (Arab, Barb) blood was added to make the horse lighter and faster, and by the seventeenth century the Holstein was so well thought of that it was being sold abroad.

Yorkshire Coach Horse blood, and a touch of Thoroughbred, was infused in the nineteenth century to give extra height and quality.

Today's Holsteiner usually stands in excess of 16 hands high. It is a handsome riding horse of impressive appearance, up to weight and with exceptionally good movement. Christine Stueckelberger's famous world champion dressage horse, Granat, was a Holstein, but representatives of the breed are also frequently seen on German three-day-event (e.g. Madrigal, Ladalco) and show jumping (e.g. Holstein Meteor) international teams.

All solid colours are permissible, but the classics are bay and brown.

HUÇUL

A strong, primitive pony of the Tarpan type, the Huçul has more refinement about it (oriental blood?) than its presumed Tarpan ancestry would suggest. Nevertheless there are those who believe its origin to be so pure that they call it the Forest Tarpan.

It comes from the Carpathian Mountains area of Poland, where it has been used for generations as a mountain pack pony and as a farm worker. It is usually dun or bay, stands 12.1-13 hands high and is sensible and hardy. *Not illustrated.*

ICELAND

Iceland was first settled by the Vikings in 871AD and until that time no animal larger than the Arctic fox was to be found in this glacial, lava-ridden land. The Norsemen brought ponies, probably from Norway and the northernmost Scottish islands, in their open boats. These ponies adapted well to Iceland's harsh conditions and, apart from an early and disastrous attempt to introduce speedy Eastern blood - causing the degeneration of the hardy Iceland breed for many years - no new horse blood has entered Iceland for over a thousand years. Indeed, such introduction of foreign blood was forbidden by an Act of Parliament in 931.

The Iceland Pony (12-13.2 hands high) is a self-reliant, independent little animal, quick to make its own assessment of a situation and aggressive

enough to stand its ground when threatened. In the very early days of settlement the Norsemen, starved of satisfaction for their blood-lust by the absence of game animals, matched their riderless ponies in horse fights. Owners were expected to assist their ponies in these contests, proving just as likely as their ponies to be savaged by the opponents.

Iceland Ponies have a remarkable homing instinct. They can be ridden for great distances by a borrower and, when loosed, will directly find their own way home. They are, of necessity, good all-rounders and have developed five gaits instead of the usual four: the walk, trot and gallop – plus the *skeid*, a short sprint at high speed, and the *tolt*, a running walk.

INDONESIAN PONIES

Several variations of pony are indigenous to the islands of Indonesia. By contrast to the Iceland Pony, which has learned to live in climates far too cold and fodder-less for ordinary animals, these little Indonesian Ponies have adapted themselves to working in tropical heat. Their sweaty climate ensures that they do not carry much flesh. Indonesian ponies are mostly small and scraggy, poor specimens of horseflesh when compared to their temperate-pasture cousins.

Appearance notwithstanding, Indonesia's ponies are important to their country's economy. They are widely used in agriculture and are, furthermore, still one of Indonesia's principal means of transport.

Indonesian ponies are very similar, though there is a slight variation in type from island to island:

The **Java Pony**, around 12.2 hands high and scrawny enough to make a horseman wince, is remarkable for its strength and tirelessness under the enervating tropic sun. It will work all day pulling *sados*, the two-wheeled traps used for taxi service, and is also used on farms.

The **Bali Pony**, 12-13 hands high and a bit, is as relentless as steel wire and often works as a pack pony. It is a primitive type, commonly having dun colouring with dark points and dorsal stripe and occasionally the upright mane of the primeval pony.

The **Sumba Pony**, closely related to the **Sumbawa** of a neighbouring island, is ridden bareback and

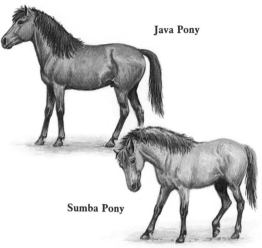

Java Pony

Sumba Pony

reinless in dancing competitions judged on elegance and lightness of foot; while the **Sandalwood**, named for Sumba's joint-biggest export (the other is ponies), runs in bareback racing and, curiously, rarely sweats.

The **Batak**, which has been improved with Arab blood, is handsomer, sweet to handle and cheap to keep.

The **Gayoe** is heavier-built and lacks the Batak's fire and speed.

The **Timor** is the smallest of the Indonesian variations. It stands only some 11 hands high. It

Timor Pony

comes from the island of Timor, the most southerly of Indonesia's islands and the nearest to the Australian mainland.

Timor ponies have been exported to Australia and New Zealand, where they are much admired for their commonsense (some horse authorities have been sufficiently impressed to call it wisdom). Their willingness and endurance are also legendary: sure-footed and exceptionally agile, the little Timor will carry a full-grown man all day on a cattle round-up.

Almost needless to say, they are beloved as children's ponies.

Timor ponies are usually dark in colour, though some exist which have a cream mane and tail, or even cream spots.

IOMUD

The Iomud originates in Soviet Central Asia. It is a small, sinewy horse, standing only 14.2-15 hands high, and is a strain of the great Turkoman, or Turkmene, horse of the USSR. It is most often grey in colour, though it can be chestnut or bay, and its coat has the fine, metallic sheen peculiar to horses of the USSR. It is an adaptable horse, and is bold and enduring.

It is not as fleet-footed as its near relative the Akhal-Teké, but it shows more Arab blood and, as expected from its looks, more stamina. A very adaptable horse on any terrain, it is untiring in distance races.

IRISH DRAUGHT HORSE

A very strong animal with massive bone on a lean body, this stolid horse is so powerful that, apart from the absence of feather on its heels and its alert air, it might be classified as a coldblood. It stands 15-17 hands high and is invaluable for all types of work from heavyweight hunting to hauling.

The Irish Draught has a pleasing dash about it. When crossed with a Thoroughbred or other quality lightweight horse – usually with the cross erring heavily on the lighter-weight side – it gives rise to notable eventers and show jumpers with bottomless stamina.

Any solid colour is acceptable in the breed, though it is usually chestnut, grey, bay or brown.

ITALIAN HEAVY DRAUGHT

Quite a fine horse when compared with the cumbersome draught horses of northern Europe, this horse shows the classic Italian colouring of liver chestnut with blonde mane, tail and feather. It is a refinement of the Breton heavy horse, crossed onto lighter breeds from the Tirol, and is faster and more active than most heavy horses. Formerly the mainstay of Italian agriculture, it is now usually bred for meat. It stands 15-16 hands high and is willing and intelligent.

JAF

A tough, wiry horse, a typical product of a harsh mountain-desert country, the Jaf has evolved in the mountainous Kurdistan region of Iran. It is a spirited animal with the classic oriental appearance of a saddle horse of Arab type.

The Jaf's feet are as hard as cobblestones and it has great powers of endurance. It is a fine riding horse, standing 15 hands high or more, and is usually chestnut, brown, bay or grey. *Not illustrated.*

JUTLAND

Dark chestnut, in most cases, with blonde mane, tail and feather, this heavy draught horse comes from Denmark's Jutland Island. Its head is plain, with long ears, but it has a kindly eye and a general expression of gentleness. The neck is short and crested, set on a massive, deep-chested front. The body is long and stout, with an exceptional depth of girth which exceeds its length of leg. There is less feather on this horse's heels than is usual in a draught horse.

It originally became established as a war horse of the middle ages, easily carrying the heavily-armoured knights of that day, but, like all Great Horses of those times, was not fast or nimble enough for later cavalry needs. 'Improved' with solid Suffolk Punch blood from eastern England, it became the most useful horse in Danish agriculture. It is very gentle and kind and stands 15-16 hands high. *Not illustrated.*

KABARDIN

A small (about 15 hands high), nice-looking, lightweight horse from the northern Caucasian Mountains, the Kabardin has adapted itself since time beyond mind to hazardous ground. It is prized for its sure-footedness and its willingness to tread apparently impossible mountain tracks. It came into being in response to the needs of tough, nomadic tribesmen who travelled on it, and who ate its flesh and drank its blood when hungry. Karabakh, Arab and Turkoman blood seem to have added to its fire.

Today's best Kabardin horses are bred at Russia's Malokarachaev and Malkin Studs. They are fine saddle and harness horses.

KARABAIR

There are three variations of Karabair: the Harness, which is long-backed and strong, the Saddle, which is fast and elegant, and the Saddle/Harness, somewhere between the two. In each case the horse has the athletic, clean-legged, low-bodied look of a fine Russian horse capable of intelligent travel over demanding distances.

The fact that this 14.1-15.3 hands high horse is of ancient mountain lineage is probably of little consequence to Russian horse lovers who, unlike their western counterparts, care less how a horse is bred and more about whether it meets their needs. The intelligent, athletic Karabair does most things

well. Crossed with Thoroughbreds, it excels in modern equestrian sport.

KARABAKH

This fiery mountain pony, roughly 14 hands high, is a light riding animal of great antiquity. It has lived in the Karabakh Mountains for at least the last 1500 years, and the best stock is presently widely crossed with small Arab horses. In its turn it has influenced other Russian breeds, the Don especially.

The coat colour of the Karabakh is dun, bay or chestnut, usually with a pronounced golden sheen. Unfortunately, the breed is now becoming rare.

KATHIAWARI AND MARWARI PONIES

These differently-labelled animals are in fact so alike that there is nothing but repetition to be gained by treating them as separate breeds. The Kathiawari comes from the Kathiawari Peninsula on the north-west coast of India, while the Marwari comes from the nearby province of Rajputana.

These ponies descend from 'indigenous' stock – that is to say from stock existing before any Western recorder found them – which doubtless arrived on the hoof many centuries ago, probably in Mongolian Pony form. These ancestors are thought to have interbred with a cargo of Arab horses allegedly running wild after a shipwreck on India's west coast.

The less aristocratic of the two Marwari and Kathiawari ancestors, the aforementioned 'indigenous' pony, is still found all over India. It looks a wretched bag of bones, very narrow, standing roughly 13 hands high, but it is as tough as a goat.

Kathiawari ponies are on the tall side, standing averagely 14.2 hands high. Light-framed and thin, they are hardy and able to live on next to nothing. Along with their plus for physical toughness goes a minus for uncertain temper. Like many poorly-fed ponies, they have a tendency to sickle hocks.

The unique feature of the Kathiawari/Marwari, and one which makes it easily recognizable, is its ears. These point so sharply inwards that, when pricked, they almost touch.

KAZAKH

The hardy Steppe pony of Kazakhstan in Russia was for centuries the mainstay of nomadic tribes. Seventh-century excavations show that Kazakh men were buried with their ponies, no doubt after depending upon them for decades not only for transport but for food and drink in a harsh environment.

The enriching blood of Don, Orlov, Russian Trotter and Thoroughbred stallions has made today's Kazakh strains taller (average 14.1 hands high) and rounder. Cheap to run, because they can still pick an adequate living from near-desert terrain, today they are usually bred for meat. *Not illustrated.*

KLADRUBER

At 16.2-17.2 hands high the Kladruber is a taller, but otherwise almost identical, version of its forerunner, the Andalusian. It is a magnificent carriage horse, showing itself off with pride and ceremony. The famous Kladruby Greys – teams of up to 16-in-hand, usually without postillion riders to help the coachman – still draw the Czechoslovakian State Coach on ceremonial occasions.

Kladrubers have been bred in Czechoslovakia since the Emperor Maximilian II founded a stud in the 16th century at Kladruby, in what was then Bohemia. The Emperor began his stud with imported Andalusian horses but the strain has gradually grown bigger.

KNABSTRUP

Standing just under 16 hands high, the Knabstrup, from Denmark, looks as if a giant had shaken out his pen on its hide. It dates from the Napoleonic Wars, when a spotted mare named Flaebehoppen was bought from a Spanish army officer and crossed with a Frederiksborg stallion. The resultant offspring, all spotted, became extremely popular as striking-looking riding horses and as circus animals. Unfortunately, too much attention has been paid in recent times to spots and not enough to type, and so the physical characteristics other than the coat colour are no longer uniform.

KONIK

This robust, well-proportioned Polish pony has been as important to the lowland farmers of its native land as its near-relative the Huçul was to the hill farmers of that country. In addition, its influence has been felt by most of the modern breeds of Polish and Russian horses and ponies.

The Konik, whose name means 'small horse', stands just over 13 hands high and is a willing, good-natured beast, easy to train and with an unusually long life span. Of all breeds in existence today it probably bears the greatest likeness to its ancestor the Tarpan, both in physical appearance and

in ability to thrive on poor fare (though not in independent mulishness).

All shades of dun coat colour clothe the Konik, often with dorsal stripe and dark points. Some ponies are said to grow white winter coats.

KUSTANAIR

Interest on the part of the Imperial Russian cavalry in the latter part of the nineteenth century stimulated the improvement of the small, hardy ponies which ran in herds in the harsh climate of Kazakhstan. Good food and care increased their natural height quite quickly from some 13 hands high to over 14 hands.

Interbreeding with Don and Thoroughbred stallions and with the now-extinct Strelets horse brought the Kustanair's height to just over 15 hands and resulted in a hard, handsome horse with short legs and plenty of bone – a horse well able to withstand the rigours of the Kustanair region of north-west Kazakhstan, for which it is named.

Three types of Kustanair have been evolved, in accordance with the needs of its homeland. There is the Steppe type, which is massive-bodied and is useful in agriculture and in harness, the Saddle type, which is light and airy, and the Basic, which is somewhere between the two and suits both purposes.

The Kustanair is a good mover. It is an intelligent, adaptable horse with great stamina. Its predominant colours are chestnut and bay, though grey is occasionally seen. *Not illustrated.*

LATVIAN HARNESS HORSE

The Latvian Harness Horse is an all-purpose breed popular throughout the Soviet Union. There are three basic types (and no doubt many intermediate variations): in the south, by far the most popular area for this horse, the Latvian appears as a powerful draught animal standing close under 15 hands high and able to do all kinds of heavy farm work, while in the north there is a taller harness type and also a lighter type with less bone, for riding, which looks more like a trotter than a draught horse.

Indigenous to Latvia since before recorded memory, this was a basic coldblood Forest type before human 'improvers' got at it with extensive warm

blood crossing. It is a physically hard, sensible horse and a hard worker.

LIMOUSIN HALFBRED

France excels in producing quality halfbred horses, and the Limousin Halfbred is no exception. The original Limousin, the medieval French riding horse said to be partly based on Barb stock abandoned in France by the Muslims in the eighth century, has been crossed for some hundreds of years with Thoroughbreds and Arabs until today it is to all extent and purposes little short of a purebred Anglo-Arab. It stands around 16 hands high and is usually coloured chestnut or bay. *Not illustrated.*

LIPIZZANER

The great white horses of the Spanish Riding School of Vienna have been more cherished as a breed, and for longer, than any other kind of horse. Their origins are Andalusian (hence the 'Spanish' name of the school), while the name Lipizzaner comes from the stud founded in 1580 at Lipizza by the Archduke Charles II of Austria.

The Lipizza stud began with nine stallions and 24 mares imported from Andalusia. However, at Piber, another famous Austrian stud, Andalusians were crossed with other breeds of similar Spanish ancestry which had proved themselves in other parts of Europe. Kladrubers were introduced from the

Emperor Maximilian II's stud in Czechoslovakia, as were the much-admired Neapolitan horses from Italy. (The Neapolitan is now extinct. It was an important breed for the cavalry of the middle ages and was mainly of Andalusian blood mixed with a little Barb and Arab to give it swiftness and agility).

Outside bloodlines – those of the Fredriksborg and the Arab – were brought in, and the best horses at Lipizza, Piber and Kladruby were frequently interbred. Yet of all this mixing and matching it seems that only one animal, the white Arabian stallion Siglavy, who was foaled in 1810, put a permanent stamp on the Lipizza line.

In times of war, Lipizzaners have been evacuated before and at the expense of humans, always returning to the area in which they flourish best. After the collapse of the Hapsburg Empire, when Lipizza became part of Italy, the Austrian Lipizzaners were re-established in their present home at Piber.

The Airs Above the Ground, the complex movements for which the Lipizzaners are renowned, are extremely advanced medieval war manoeuvres. The *capriole*, in which the horse leaps vertically upward from a standstill and kicks out, got the rider out of many a tight spot when he was hemmed in by his enemies. The *levade*, in which the horse crouches and rears (*illustrated on page 148*), helped the rider to stab his opponent from above.

It takes about seven years to train a Lipizzaner to perform such sophisticated war manoeuvres, which would not be possible at all if the horses were not extremely intelligent and sweet-natured.

The levade

Lipizzaners look very much like Andalusians, though they may be slightly smaller and their faces are often straight. Their presence, if possible, is even greater.

The White Horses of Vienna, slow to mature, are long-lived and often work well into their thirties. They are so much accepted as white that it seems strange when, as occasionally happens, a bay one appears.

LITHUANIAN HEAVY DRAUGHT

Placid to the point of indolence, this massive piece of horsepower was developed earlier this century to

serve the agricultural needs of the Russian Baltic
states. Powerful Swedish Ardennes stallions were
bred onto the hardy Zhmud mares of the locality. The
new breed was registered in 1963.

Although it stands little more than 15 hands high,
the Lithuanian gives an impression of enormous
power. It is usually chestnut, often with flaxen mane
and tail. It moves well at a walk (speedier gaits are
not required) and thrives on simple food.

LOKAI

The Lokai, from Russia, stands not much over 14
hands high, though its proportions suggest a much
taller horse. It was originally bred, some three or four

centuries ago, by the Lokai tribe of Uzbekistan, who used it as a mountain pack pony.

Cross-breeding with Akhal-Teké, Arab and Thoroughbred blood has made the Lokai's Steppe pony ancestry barely visible. Nonetheless the Lokai retains hereditary gifts of endurance and sure-footedness. Its colours are usually bay, grey or chestnut, sometimes with a metallic sheen to the coat.

LUSITANO

This splendid Portuguese saddle horse is of obscure origin. It has existed in Portugal for several hundred years and its mettlesome but compact appearance, coupled with its predominantly grey coat (though it can be any solid colour), indicate a very close relationship with its great Iberian neighbour, the Andalusian. A touch of Arab blood is also a possibility.

Formerly a cavalry horse, the Lusitano is today the favoured mount of the Portuguese bullfighter. In Portugal, bullfighting is a ceremonial art in which the bull is played with in a series of classical manoeuvres but is not killed, and in which it is thought disgraceful if a horse is injured. The *rejoneadores* perform entirely from horseback and train their mounts to high standards of *haute école* so that the obedience and agility of the horses is very precise.

Lusitanos possess both the courage to face a charging bull and the dexterity to slip aside at the last second.

MANGALARGA

An attractive Brazilian riding horse, the Mangalarga presents a more elegant appearance than its famous relative, the Criollo. It is lighter-framed than the Argentinian horse and has longer cannon bones and pasterns, no doubt because it is the result of breeding Andalusian and Altér-Real stallions with Criollo mares. Nonetheless, it stands, in general, a shade under 15 hands high.

The most desirable Mangalargas display an unusual, comfortable gait called the *marcha*. This is a pleasant, rocking movement somewhere between a trot and a canter. This horse's colours are chestnut, bay, roan and grey.

MANIPURI

From the Assam state of Manipur, where polo is claimed to have been introduced by the King of

Manipur in the 7th century, this is the original polo pony as far as Westerners are concerned. English tea planters, working in Assam in the 1850s, took to the game enthusiastically. The ponies they rode were the tiny (11-13 hands high) Manipuris, spirited little beasts by tropical climate standards. Claims are made that they are a mixture of Mongolian and Arab blood and that they were the mounts of the all-conquering State cavalry which once terrorized northern Burma.

MAREMMANA

Italy's largest indigenous riding horse, the Maremmana (also called **Maremma**) is used by the country's

153

mounted police. Its calm and patient nature also suits it to light agricultural work, while, being active and intelligent, it is a popular ride with the *butteri* (cowboys) who herd the cattle. These are quite a variety of uses for one heavyish saddle/light draught animal – they demonstrate the Maremmana's versatility. It has additional qualities of endurance and being able to thrive on poor fare.

Like all native Italian horses it tends to be chestnut with flaxen mane and tail, but other solid colours are seen. It stands 15.3 hands high. *Not illustrated.*

METIS TROTTER

Russia's attempt to improve the Orlov Trotter, this is a cross between the native breed and good American Standardbreds. The breeding aims to single out the good qualities of both parent lines but, being begun only in the 1950s, offspring of predictable performance are still uncertain.

Height averages 15.3 hands and the commonest colours are grey, bay, black and chestnut. The new Metis Trotter is a tough, brave horse of characteristic trotter conformation, though there is still a tendency to an upright shoulder which hampers the movement of the forelegs. *Not illustrated.*

MONGOLIAN PONY

One of the most ancient of all pony types, the Mongolian is found all over the mountainous regions

of southern Asia. It is a thickset animal, very hardy and capable of grafting itself a living in the most stringent of pastureland.

There are no fixed standards for this type of pony, which in general shows its scrubby, Przewalski Horse, origins. It is simply a useful indigenous animal, standing from 12.2 hands high up to horse height, and in colour dun, brown, bay or black. Mongolians are used for every task, right down to the supply of milk or meat for their masters. Their ungainly, small-eyed heads and short, thick necks are rightly reckoned as of little moment when compared with their deep chests, strong, short backs and iron-like legs and feet.

More refined types exist, standing up to 15 hands high, where the grassland is good and where quality Russian blood has been intermixed.

MORGAN

One of the best and most intelligent of all saddle horses, this astonishing American breed is so sensitive to its rider's needs that the horseman has to be fast off the ball to live up to it.

Morgan horses of our acquaintance have shown at least the following unhorselike characteristics:

1 A working stallion displayed himself in classic Morgan pose (legs extended fore and aft, head high and eyes unwavering into camera) while humans walked to and fro under his belly.

2 A Morgan mare challenged an experienced rider towards inventive movements beyond the rider's knowledge, yet half an hour later gave a riding lesson to a five-year-old child.

3 An old mare, prepared in the country for a London exhibition of the Morgan's skills, became puzzled by the city's white road markings. Her rider had not thought to teach her that these had no significance for horses.

All Morgans are descended from one prepotent sire, Justin Morgan, an animal of astonishing versatility and intelligence who was foaled in Massachusetts in 1793. Claims have been made that he was by a Thoroughbred racehorse, but it is much more likely that he came from Welsh Cob stock.

Modern Morgans are said to resemble Justin Morgan. They stand 14-15.2 hands high and are black, brown, bay or chestnut. They are wonderful

harness and saddle horses, very smooth to sit on and with dramatic, high-actioned, floating paces. Like the Welsh Cob, they are strong and hardy and have great powers of endurance.

MURAKOZ

This heavy farm worker stems from the banks of the river Mura in southern Hungary, where quality Hungarian stallions, Ardennais, Percherons and Norikers were bred with selected local mares. It is a very powerful horse, usually chestnut with flaxen mane and tail, and it stands about 16 hands high.

The Murakoz is an active, co-operative animal. It became so popular in its native land that in the first

157

part of this century one out of every five horses in Hungary was a Murakoz. Regrettably, its numbers are now decimated.

MUSTANG

This is the name given to the feral horse of the USA's Wild West, a tough and intractable character of middle height (usually 14-15 hands high) which used to run in herds on America's great plains but which has now been shot down almost to extinction because of the damage it did to pastureland (and also because it was a cheap form of dog meat).

Horses are not indigenous to America. This one escaped from the fine Spanish mounts brought over by the Conquistadores. Survival in the wild made it

degenerate into a light-framed scrub horse. It was sometimes captured and ridden by the Indians, and was also the first cow pony.

It is variously called **Mustang**, **Bronco** and **Cayuse**. Few are left today, excepting the independent Bucking Broncos of rodeo fame.

NATIVE MEXICAN

This horse comes from the same origins as the Mustang, but some are of better quality because of more recent interbreeding with Spanish horses and with the Criollo. It it a lean-framed saddle horse standing roughly 15 hands high, a basic scrub type which has adapted to a hostile climate. *Not illustrated*.

...have been running wild in the area of
...shire known as the New Forest for more than
...9 years. In early times this area extended almost
...s far west as Exmoor and Dartmoor, so it is likely
that this most easy to train of all British ponies
contains quite a lot of blood from those two more
identifiable breeds.

Any kind of pony has been allowed to run in the
Forest provided that the owner lived within the
Forest's boundaries and owned Rights of Common
Pasture, and because of this the New Forest Pony is
not instantly recognizable as a breed. It ranges in
height from a maximum of 14.2 hands high down to
around 12 hands and can be any colour except
piebald, skewbald or cream with blue eyes. The
breed's unifying factor lies more in its character than

in its appearance: because it has always lived in an environment with humans around it, it is exceptionally easy to handle, and because – at least in recent times – it is familiar with traffic from its birth, it is usually quietly-behaved on modern roads.

Over the years attempts have been made to improve the New Forest pony by loosing Welsh, Arab, Thoroughbred and Hackney stallions to run with the herds. These attempts were not always successful, as some of the progeny failed to survive on the sparse winter grass.

The Thoroughbred stallion Marske, sire of the unbeaten racehorse Eclipse, covered New Forest mares from 1765-1769, while from 1852-1860 Queen Victoria sent the splendid Arab stallion Zorah to run with the ponies. Highland and Fell sires were also introduced to lend substance to the native pony breed.

161

No outside blood has been permitted since 1938. The modern New Forest is categorized into Type A, a slightly-built child's pony standing up to 13.2 hands high, and the solider Type B, standing up to 14.2 hands high and suitable for a small adult to ride.

NEW KIRGHIZ

The old Kirghiz horse (or rather pony, as it stood below 13.2 hands high) has been bred by nomads in the high mountain areas of Tien Shan in the Russian province of Kirghizia since time out of mind. It was used for pack and haulage work and also for the production of milk. Extensive outcrossing with Don and Thoroughbred stallions began in the 1930s and has resulted in a strong and handsome saddle and

harness type standing around 15 hands high and bearing little resemblance to the original Kirghiz. The New Kirghiz has, however, retained its forerunner's hardiness and great stamina.

NONIUS

This medium/heavy Hungarian horse is believed to descend from a prepotent French stallion called Nonius which was foaled in Normandy about 1810 from a Norman mare by an English halfbred sire. It is a forerunner of the Furioso and looks very much like it.

The Nonius is a compact horse with a free stride and a willing nature. It stands around 15 hands high and is popular as a riding or driving animal.

NORTH SWEDISH

This long-bodied, short-legged coldblood, with a rather large head and longish ears, has lived in northern Scandinavia since antiquity and is a visible reminder of the primitive Forest horse of north Europe. It has the Forest's large, round feet. Its mane and tail are thick, and there is feather on its heels. It is frugal and long-lived and has an excellent constitution. Farmers and lumbermen value it for its kindness and its willingness to work.

The North Swedish stands around 15.2 hands high and is an energetic mover with a long, clean stride. Døle-Gudbrandsdal stallions, which must be of the

same parentage, have been used to regulate the stock since 1890, when the North Swedish breed society was formed. Log-pulling tests and stringent veterinary examinations have since ensured that only the best horses are bred from. The result is a splendid horse which is easy to handle and cheap to feed.

NORTH SWEDISH TROTTER

The North Swedish is a brilliant natural trotter with inspiring length of stride. The lighter-framed animals, predictably, are the fastest, and it is these which have tempted their owners onto the trotting racetrack. The best have been selectively interbred for trotting and provide good sport in the harsh climates near the Arctic Circle, but they cannot compete for speed with the trotters of more clement climates. *Not illustrated.*

OLDENBURG

This is the tallest and heaviest of the German warmbloods. At 16.2-17.2 hands high, tall even by heavy draught standards, it is a strong, all-purpose saddle horse with good conformation and is a splendid horse for a tall or heavy rider. It carries itself well, has an imposing presence and is more of an athlete than its size would suggest, excelling in show jumping and dressage (albeit often doing best when outcrossed with a less massive breed).

It is a precocious horse which matures early. Its character mixes boldness with kindness, backed by

stalwart common sense. Colours are any solid colour, but black, brown and bay are most common.

This imposing creature has been flourishing since at least the 17th century. It was first bred as a quality coach horse, by crossing imported Andalusian and Neapolitan animals with draught horses of the old Friesian type. It must have been indeed a powerful animal, very serviceable on the rutted roads before tarmac was known.

Later additions of Thoroughbred, Hanoverian, Norman and Cleveland Bay blood lightened its frame and speeded it up as a coaching horse, and Thoroughbred and Anglo-Norman blood has since been added to suit the Oldenburg more to riding uses.

ORLOV TROTTER

Trotting is extremely popular in the USSR, where more than 30,000 Orlovs are bred at 34 State studs. There are five basic types of Orlov, showing slight differences to suit the climatic variations of this vast nation. They average around 15.3 hands high and are mostly grey, black or bay.

They originated at the Orlov Stud near Moscow, through the efforts of Count Alexius Grigorievich Orlov, who began breeding trotters in 1777. Very many bloodlines have gone into the modern Orlov, which, although somewhat slower then the American Standardbred, has great presence and provides good sport.

PALOMINO

Palomino is not a breed but a colour. The coat colour should be that of a gold coin, the mane and tail white, and the eyes dark. White markings are not permitted except on the face or legs. This colouring appears in horses and ponies of many sizes and shapes, but has proved a difficult one to breed true.

In Great Britain it is a colouring sought after in children's ponies but is seldom found in riding horses. In America, the only country to try to establish Palominos as a breed of recognizable physical type, the reverse is true. The classic American Palomino stands 14.1-16 hands high and has the physique of a Quarter Horse or Morgan.

PASO FINO

A small, quality riding horse, 14.3 hands high, this breed evolved in Puerto Rico and equatorial South America from Conquistadore stock and is now popular in the United States. It exhibits three comfortable four-beat gaits, all of them natural to it and not needing to be taught. The slowest and most collected of these gaits is the *paso fino*; the *paso corto* covers long distances at a steady pace and there is also the faster *paso largo*.

All colours are seen. The Paso Fino is a willing horse with a strong body and hard legs. It carries itself gaily.

PERCHERON

One of the most famous of all the heavy horse breeds, the great French Percheron has a surprising elegance which has caused it to be likened to an overgrown Arab. It does, indeed, contain Oriental blood, mixed over many centuries in the Perche region of France with local heavy draught breeds. It stands 15.2-17 hands high and is grey or black. There is little feather on its feet.

This magnificent heavy horse, probably the most popular in the world, has enjoyed a great following in Britain and the United States. Now that its agricultural day is done, it is sad to see that today it is usually bred for meat.

PERUVIAN STEPPING HORSE

This horse, also called the **Peruvian Paso**, is a curious mover to European eyes – yet its action seems similar to the medieval gait called the *amble*. The *paso* (step) of this small horse can carry a rider untiringly for hours. It is a gait unknown in any other modern horse in that the forelegs paddle out sideways rather like a swimmer's arms, while the hindlegs, held low under the body, move forward in a long, straight line. It makes the horse extremely comfortable to sit on, while averaging 11 miles (18 km) per hour.

Stepping Horses have typical Criollo personalities, showing great endurance. They are usually bay or chestnut and stand around 15 hands high.

PINTO

Also called the **Paint Horse**, this type of horse is traditionally associated in the USA with Indian ponies. In Britain, where the coat colour is called *Piebald* if black and white and *Skewbald* if brown and white, the association is with gipsy caravans.

It is a colour rather than a breed, though the Pinto Horse Association of America has tried to make the Pinto conform to recognizable physical characteristics, both of horse and pony size, and so far approves of four types. These are the Stock type, looking like a Quarter Horse, the Hunter type, of predominantly Thoroughbred cast, the Pleasure type with Arab/Morgan looks, and the Saddle type, bred in the flamboyant style of the plantation horse of the southeastern States.

Horses with white splashes on a dark coat (*above right*) are called Overo, while those with dark splashes on a white base (*below right*) are called Tobiano. Horses composed fairly evenly of black and white patches are called Piebald in the USA (as indeed *any* horse with black and white patches is called Piebald in Great Britain), while horses whose coats are composed of roughly even amounts of brown and white patches are called Skewbald by Americans – and of course by the British, who make no allowance for dominant patches of colour anyway.

If this sounds confusing, well, yes it is! The confusion arises because Americans are more particular than the British in variations of colour names.

Overo Pinto

Tobiano Pinto

PINZGAUER NORIKER

This solid workhorse from Austria and Germany is also known as the **South German Coldblood**. It stands over 16 hands high and is a plain-looking horse with a gentle expression.

The Pinzgauer Noriker is an ancient breed, said to have been known under Roman rule in the Kingdom of Noricum (modern Austria). 'Pinzgauer' refers to the Pinzgau district of Austria.

A mountain breed, it is handier than most other horses for steep hill country. Colours are usually bay and chestnut, often with flaxen mane and tail. Spotted coats, dun and skewbald are also seen.

PLATEAU PERSIAN

Exquisite small riding horses have been produced in the hostile mountain country of Iran's central plateau since before the time of Christ. These horses are very like the desert Arabian and show much the same elegance and fire. They came about through the same ruthless natural selection process, grew up in a similar environment scant of food and water, were fed a diet by their masters which was often meagre (dates were better than nothing, and sometimes horses even ate dried camel flesh), and learned to endure extremities of heat by day and of cold by night.

Even today they are often the mounts of nomadic tribes who scratch a living from rough mountain country. Their ancestors are the sure-footed and hardy strains of the age-old Shirazi, Quashquai, Basseri, Bakhtiari and Persian Arab horses.

In 1978 these horses were grouped together by the Royal Horse Society of Iran under the single heading Plateau Persian. Two of the most popular strains are the Darashouri (*page 85*) and the Jaf (*page 134*).

PLEVEN

A robust Anglo-Arab horse from Bulgaria, this breed stands about 15.2 hands high and is bright chestnut in colour. It is now widely bred in its homeland, where it is popular as an all-round saddle animal and is sometimes also used in agriculture. The Pleven is a natural jumper. *Not illustrated.*

POITEVIN

The Poitevin is a large, gaunt coldblood, standing nearly 17 hands high. It was originally imported to drain the marshes around Poitiers, in France, because of its strength and partly because its huge, flat feet stopped it from sinking into the mire. It has survived as a breed because Poitevin mares, when mated with tall jackasses, produce big, strong mules.

The Poitevin is otherwise undistinguished. Mentally it is thick-witted and lethargic. It came from the flatlands of northern Europe and is reminiscent of the ancient Forest type of horse.

Colours are primeval. It is usually dun, but can be bay or brown.

PONY OF THE AMERICAS

The Pony of the Americas is one of the very few breeds to be certain of where it came from – doubtless because it is one of the most recent breeds to go on record. It is a charming child's pony. It came about in 1954 when Mr Leslie L. Boomhower of Mason City, Iowa, crossed a Shetland stallion with an Appaloosa mare. In the spring of the following year a very attractive miniature colt was born, which Mr Boomhower called Black Hand.

Black Hand's descendants are all Appaloosa-coloured. They are quality ponies, looking like tiny Quarter Horses crossed with Arabs. They stand 11.2-13 hands high, or a little over, and make gentle and versatile mounts for young riders.

PREZWALSKI'S HORSE

Equus przewalskii przewalskii Poliakov, to give it its scientific name, is more famous as the Asiatic or Mongolian Wild Horse. It is an intractable little animal which has survived – just about – without submission to man, despite the fact that humans have taken away most of its best grazing grounds and have driven it on to very limited, barren land.

It stands 12-14.2 hands high and has a dun-coloured coat, often with dark points. It has a mealy muzzle, and usually the same mealy-light colouring around the eyes and under the belly. Its mane is short and upright and there is no forelock. Its tail is long and thickly-growing, though scraggy at the top. Usually it has a dark dorsal stripe, and sometimes there are zebra markings on its legs.

It has a large, heavy head on a short neck. The ears are long and pointed, the eyes small and set high up, and the face is straight in profile or convex.

It is one of the three primeval types from which all horse and pony breeds descend. It still runs wild, though in regrettably small numbers, in the Mountains of the Yellow Horse (Tachin Schara Nuru Mountains) on the western edge of the Gobi Desert. In 1881 a Russian explorer, Colonel Przewalski, after whom the horse is named, discovered a small herd and brought it to the attention of the outside world.

Przewalski's Horse – in actuality a pony – has scarcely altered since the Ice Age. Numerous opportunities for interbreeding with other types of

horse must have arisen over the millenia but the little Mongolian horse remained unchanged, partly because runaway domestic mares are unable to survive the extreme conditions in which it lives and partly because the stallions are alert and extremely aggressive and will attack and kill invading males long before they get near the herds.

Over the centuries it has been hunted to near-extinction by hungry tribesmen. The few remaining herds are now protected by the Mongolian, Russian and Chinese governments, but only some 50 animals are believed still to run in their native habitat.

Probably the greatest hope for the continuing future existence of this only true wild horse lies in the 200 or so which survive in zoos around the world.

RHINELAND HEAVY DRAUGHT

Massive and very muscular, this gentle-natured work horse stands 16-17 hands high and is chestnut or red roan, often with blonde mane and tail or black points.

Also known as the **Rhenish-German**, the Rhineland Heavy Draught was developed about 100 years ago to meet demands of agriculture and heavy industry. Quick to mature and economical to feed, by the early twentieth century it had become the most popular and most numerous heavy horse breed in Germany.

Several breeds contributed to its evolution but its principal ancestor was the Belgian Draught Horse.

RUSSIAN HEAVY DRAUGHT

Founded at about the same time as the Rhineland Heavy Draught, and for the same reasons, this is the smallest of the heavy draught breeds. It averages just over 14.2 hands high and is usually chestnut, roan or bay.

A very pleasant horse to work with, being sweet-tempered and lively, it has an unusually long working life. The breed is quick to mature, having grown very nearly to its full height by 18 months of age, and so fertile is it that stallions and mares are often still at stud when well into their twenties.

SABLE ISLAND

Sable Island is a barren, treeless sandbank off the coast of Nova Scotia. Winters are often severe and it is remarkable that horses should survive in this unprotected land. However, some 40 or 50 herds of scrub-type animals, standing 14-15 hands high, run wild and seem to thrive on a diet of little more than coarse grass. Most of them are chestnut (often dark), but some are black, brown, bay or grey. They are wiry and very hardy.

No one is quite sure where the ponies came from, but they are thought to have been imported from New England as part of a policy to encourage early settlers.

SALERNO

The Salerno, once a favourite of the Italian cavalry, is now declining in numbers because armies do not need it any more. It comes from the regions of Salerno and Maremma and is a high-quality saddle horse with a slightly large head and a strong body. It has good bone and an attractive conformation with prominent withers. The horse stands about 16 hands high and can be of any solid colour.

The breed is based on Neapolitan and Andalusian blood, with later additions of Thoroughbred and Arab. Though it has declined in numbers since its army heyday it is still in demand as a riding horse and shows an especial talent for show jumping.

SARDINIAN

A small, tough horse of good conformation, this is, as the name implies, an island breed. It rarely exceeds 15.2 hands high and can be smaller. Its coat is usually brown or bay.

The Sardinian is a clever horse, sure-footed and with a clean, straight action. It is an attractive riding horse which will adapt itself to most requirements, including use by mounted police. It has in the past show jumped at international level as a member of the Italian Army team.

SCHLESWIGER

Almost always chestnut, often with blonde mane and tail, this heavy draught horse takes its name from the Schleswig-Holstein region of north Germany. The breed is similar to the Danish Jutland, to which it is closely related, though it is a shade lighter and more cob-like. It was much in demand as a bus and tram horse before artificial horsepower was invented. It is placid and kind and a good mover.

The Schleswiger, also called the **Schleswig Heavy Draught**, stands 15.2-16 hands high and is dense-bodied and compact in build. Its legs are muscular and lightly feathered. It has a short, crested neck, rising from almost unnoticeable withers. The head is plain.

SHAGYA ARAB

Hungary's grey Arabian, which looks typical of the Seglawi Arab strain (the type with feminine beauty and elegance), is not a purebred in the strictest sense as some of the early foundation mares were not Arabian.

The breed began at the army stud at Bábolna, following an order in 1816 that all mares should be covered by Oriental stallions. Venereal disease decimated the stud in the 1830s, so the Bábolna commandant, Major Freiherr von Herbert, imported new blood in the form of five mares and nine stallions from the Arabian desert. The best of these was a grey called Shagya, who proved a prepotent sire. Shagyas are now used as civilian saddle horses.

SHETLAND

Arguably the most loved of all the world's ponies, the Shetland is also one of the purest of native British breeds. It has been observed in the Shetland and Orkney Islands off the northern coast of Scotland since 500 BC, at which time it apparently became domesticated.

It is a diminutive breed – the maximum permitted height is 105cm (42in) and the lowest recorded height is 65cm (26in) – and is possessed of strength out of all proportion to its size. The Shetland's physical prowess is a source of wonder to all. 'Some not so high as others prove to be the strongest,' wrote the Reverend John Brand in 1701. 'Yea there are some,

whom an able man can lift up in his arms, yet will they carry him and a woman behind him eight miles forward and as many back.' In 1820 a Shetland 90cm (36in) high is recorded as having carried a 77kg (170lb) man 64km (40 miles) in one day (but the record does not say what the man did with his long legs).

No one knows how the ponies came to be on the islands, though all agree that their small size is due to the stunting climatic conditions and the lack of available natural food.

'The Coldness of the Air, the Barrenness of the Mountains on which they feed and their hard usage may occasion to keep them so little,' thought Brand, 'for if bigger Horses be brought into the Country, their kind within a little time will degenerate; and indeed in the present case we may see the Wisdom of Providence, for their way being deep and Mossie in many places, these lighter Horses come through when the greater and heavier would sink down; and they leap over ditches very nimbly, yea up and down Mossy braes with heavy riders upon them, which I could not look upon but with Admiration.'

Shetlands protect themselves by growing winter coats of enormous thickness, by bushy tails and by manes that are so thick and long that they obscure the head and neck. In winter, when the islands are covered with snow, they climb down to the beaches and eat the seaweed blown in by the Atlantic gales.

Shetland ponies have been used for all manner of work from coal mining to carting. They are lively little ponies which adapt splendidly to today's competition driving requirements. Their size makes them ideal mounts for young children but, as their intelligence (and obviously their strength) usually exceeds that of their riders, they need to be carefully trained to obey young horsemen's wishes.

The Shetland has been exported all over the world. It is especially loved in America, where good food and a clement climate has encouraged its growth to up to 115cm (46in). Unfortunate attempts to keep the size down to that of the island original has led to gross deformities in some of the smaller American Shetlands (*see also page 44*).

All coat colours are permissible in this breed, including piebald, skewbald and dun, but dark brown and black are most common.

SHIRE

This is the tallest horse in the world and one of the most loveable. It averages 17 hands high but sometimes exceeds 18 hands; yet, despite its massive size, the Shire can be trusted to obey the wishes of the smallest child.

The Shire is a heavy work horse of which Britain is justly proud. It derives from the Old English Black

Horse, which in turn stemmed from the Great Horses which carried medieval knights in their heavy shining armour. When war horses of the heavy type became obsolete, the Shire, like many other lumbering warrior horses, was bred to become even bigger and more powerful to suit the needs of agriculture and industry. A touch of Thoroughbred blood seems to have been added, which, to some extent, would account for the present aristocratic appearance of the Shire horse.

The Shire is phenomenally strong. A splendid pair at the 1924 Wembley Exhibition, pulling against a mechanical measuring device, were recorded as able to shift a starting weight of 50 tons (50.8 tonnes), and the same pair, yoked one behind the other, moved off on a slippery wet surface with 18.5 tons (18.8 tonnes) in tow before the trace horse had even got into his collar, all the burden being borne by the horse in front.

Despite the universal decline of the heavy horse there is no danger of the Shire becoming extinct. Admired by many, it is a sure show ring attraction and is a popular puller of brewers' drays.

Colours are black, grey, brown or bay, usually with a white face and silky white feather extending downwards from the knees. Its disposition is extremely kind.

SOKOLSKY

A kindly-natured warmblood from Poland and the USSR, this sturdy workhorse has been of immense value to small farmers in its homeland. It is seen in any solid colour, though chestnut is by far the most common. It stands 15-16 hands high and is a powerful animal with a well-developed, sloping shoulder and deep chest and girth. Its back is straight and on the short side. Its legs are hard and almost devoid of feather and its feet are large and round. The head is large, with a straight face and mobile ears.

The Sokolsky adapts to almost any sort of farm work and is a good harness horse. It has a strong constitution and is frugal to keep. *Not illustrated.*

SORRAIA

A primitive type of pony, similar in type to the Tarpan, it inhabits the Sorraia river country on the western edge of Spain and is probably related to the neighbouring Portuguese Garrano.

The Sorraia stands 12.2-13 hands high, and is grey or palomino or dun with a black eel stripe down its back and zebra markings on its legs – typical colouring of a primitive breed – and, as might be expected, it is very tough and can scratch a living from the poorest of pasture. It was formerly a useful horse for Spanish smallholders but modern methods have outdated it and its numbers have greatly decreased. *Not illustrated.*

SPITI

This little Indian pony, 12 hands high, lives on the highest ranges of the Himalayan Mountains and is used as a pack pony on the narrow mountain passes.

The Spiti is a thickset pony, sure-footed and able to bear a heavy load. It is also alert, intelligent and tireless, and it might be thought a paragon of mountain ponies were not its disposition sometimes sour.

Its principle breeders are the Kanyats, for whom it earns one of their main sources of income in trade with nearby states.

SUFFOLK PUNCH

A dense, compact heavy draught horse from England's East Anglia, this is one of the purest of all the heavy breeds. It seems to have arisen naturally from local animals of the Great Horse type combined with Norfolk Trotters and Norfolk Cobs. It is easily distinguishable because, apart from being exclusively chestnut in its coat, it has no feather on its heels.

The Suffolk Punch stands 16-16.2 hands high and its body demonstrates economy of power. Its action is good at all paces, especially at the trot, and it is a long-lived horse which is cheap to feed. It is reliable in character, is gentle and is rightly very popular.

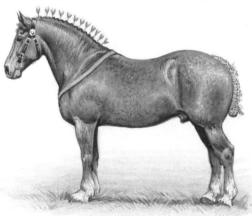

SWEDISH ARDENNES

This heavy draught horse, which looks much like the Ardennais, is a cross between that Belgian breed and the indigenous North Swedish horse. The similarity to the imported paternal line occurs because the terrain and climate of the Swedish plainlands resemble those of Belgium, though when the Ardennes is bred in colder, steeper country it becomes more agile and smaller than its normal 15.2-16 hands high.

The Swedish Ardennes can be black, bay, brown or chestnut. It is now declining in numbers. Its principal use today is for timber-hauling in areas too cold or too steep for motor vehicles.

SWEDISH WARMBLOOD

This horse comes from Flyinge, in Sweden. It is also called the **Swedish Halfbred**, due to the large amount of Thoroughbred blood in its veins.

This is a quality saddle horse, standing in excess of 16 hands high, which has been carefully built up over the past 300 years by breeding a wide range of European and Oriental riding horses onto good local mares. The original aim was to produce the perfect cavalry horse, but the end result is an outstanding civilian riding horse excelling in dressage and jumping at international level.

The usual colours for the Swedish Warmblood are chestnut, brown, bay or grey.

TARPAN

These are the last survivors of the primitive *Steppes* pony, one of the three founder types of all horses and ponies everywhere. They still live semi-wild in forest reserves near Popielno, Poland, and others are found in some zoos. Or perhaps these are not *real* Tarpans. Some people claim that the true Tarpan became extinct almost 100 years ago and that today's Tarpans are merely very close relatives.

Standing around 13 hands high, they show the classic primitive colouring of mouse dun to brown, with a dark donkey stripe down the backbone and sometimes zebra stripes on the legs. In very cold climates the winter coat is occasionally white, as happens with other wild species living in the Arctic where white is a camouflage against predators.

TCHENARAN

This is not a breed in itself but the offspring of a
Plateau Persian stallion and a Turkoman mare.
Curiously, the reverse cross of a Turkoman stallion
with a Persian mare does not produce so nice a foal,
while when Tchenaran is bred to Tchenaran the
offspring deteriorate in quality.

Bred in Iran, these are attractive saddle horses
standing around 15 hands high and possessing both
courage and stamina.

TENNESSEE WALKING HORSE

In the United States in the days of rich plantation
owners a need came about for a horse which was
purely a pleasure to ride. Plantation kings required a

horse that was was handsome and well-behaved and which would be smooth to sit on at every pace.

The Tennessee Walking Horse, bred for this purpose, carries itself gaily. It has a flowing mane and tail and an artificially-high tail carriage (caused by nicking a muscle in the tail). It has three unusual inherited gaits which make it the most comfortable ride on earth. The flat walk and the faster running walk are four-beat gaits, smooth and long-striding and with showy action, while the high rolling motion of the canter is likened to sitting on a rocking chair. The horse stands 15-16 hands high and can be any solid colour.

TERSKY

This beautifully-proportioned Russian horse, based on the old Strelets-Arab-Orlov breeds, evolved in the first half of this century at the Tersk and Stavropol studs in the northern Caucasus. More Arab blood than anything else was added to the Strelets, and also strains of Don and Kabardin.

Nearly all Terskys are silver-white in colour. They have large, expressive eyes, gay carriage and bodies which are a little fuller and rounder than those of pure-bred Arabs. Their elegant movement makes them popular in circuses, but they also excel at most equestrian sports.

These horses are compact and small, standing around 15 hands high.

THOROUGHBRED

The English Thoroughbred must be the only breed in the world to be better known by its trade name – racehorse. It was as a racehorse that it came into existence, roughly 250 years ago, and as a racehorse – the fastest horse ever known – that it goes from strength to strength today. So valuable have Thoroughbreds become that untried yearlings sometimes change hands at tens of millions of dollars, while the value of a top-class winning three-year-old colt is beyond most people's imaginings.

The Thoroughbred was by no means the first racehorse. It is merely the fastest. Horses have been raced since very ancient times: the earliest known instructions for training them appear on Hittite cuneiform tablets dating from about 3200BC. The first efforts involved starving horses of water and loosing them to see which would run first for a drink. Later they were ridden and driven (in Roman chariot races, for example).

Following the Roman occupation of Britain, racing of a minor sort took place all over Britain. There were private matches between gentlemen and there were races around the market place on public holidays. Of course, racing was not limited to Britain – in Italy, for instance, the famous *Palio*, with horses ridden bareback round the market square of Siena, has been held since the middle ages.

King James I of England was the first to emphasise the military and civil importance of a horse's speed,

as opposed to the then more common virtues of strength and suppleness. Though preferring hawking and hunting, he encouraged the sport of racing at his hunting palace in the tiny village of Newmarket in East Anglia and helped along the importation of good foreign stock to strengthen the breed.

King Charles II went one better, becoming the only English king ever to win a race with himself as jockey. That race was the Newmarket Town Plate, which was – and still is – open to any resident of Newmarket.

Such royal patronage made racing 'The Sport of Kings', but it was not until half a century later that the three great foundation sires, from whom all Thoroughbreds stem, arrived in England. They were the Darley Arabian, sent 'home' in 1704 by Thomas Darley, British Consul in Aleppo; the Byerley Turk, captured by Captain Byerley at Buda in the 1680s and ridden by him in the Battle of the Boyne; and the Godolphin Arabian, foaled in 1724 in the Yemen and eventually acquired, via a gift from the Bey of Tunis to the King of France, by Lord Godolphin. These three were bred onto the best English racing mares with such success that every modern Thoroughbred has one or all of them in its pedigree.

In racing history the principal events of the 18th century were the founding, in 1752, of the social Jockey Club, which was later to become the governing body of British racing, and the inauguration, in 1780, of the Derby by the Earl of Derby and his friend Sir Charles Bunbury (the race was namd for Derby, but Bunbury's colt, Diomed, won it).

In the 19th century racing gained such popularity

that even Parliament did not sit on Derby Day. The Derby was called the Blue Riband of the Turf and was a great event in Victorian times – an illustration of how important the fastest breed of horse on earth had become to human society.

People thronged in hundreds of thousands to the racecourse. Betting was widespread; frauds and doping abounded. Probably the coolest villain of the Turf was Francis Ignatius Coyle, who played a daring part in the Great Swindle of 1844. The Derby of that year was won by a horse entered as Running Rein, who was recognized by a previous owner as an older horse named Maccabaeus. The winning horse was objected to for being older than the statutory Derby three years and Running Rein's owner brought an action to recover the prize money. The all-important

piece of evidence was the horse, who was confined under police surveillance in his stable yard.

On the morning of the day when several veterinary surgeons were assigned to establish Running Rein's real age, Mr Coyle rode into the yard on his hack to do business with Running Rein's trainer. Afterwards he rode quietly away again through a cordon of detectives. But Mr Coyle's hack remained in the stable yard and Running Rein was never seen again.

During the first half of the 20th century Thoroughbreds became so valuable that they were, for a time, Britain's fifth-biggest export. Racehorses were sold for fabulous prices, but this trade has proved shortsighted – Britain is now having to buy back its best stock from North America for even greater sums.

The Thoroughbred stands, on average, 16 hands high but can be as small as 14.2 hands or as tall as 18 hands. It is bay, brown, black, chestnut or grey. Long legs and a streamlined body have made it supreme not only in racing but in three-day eventing, though it cannot match its Arab forebears for brains and for endurance.

TIBETAN PONY

Also called the **Nanfan**, this unprepossessing pony is nevertheless a useful and intelligent all-round friend of the people of Tibet. Although not much more than 12 hands high, it manages most agricultural tasks and also works as a pack and riding pony. It has short,

strong legs and well-shaped feet and is hardy and thrifty.

TORIC

A strong harness and general work horse of heavy cob type, the Toric comes from Estonia in the USSR and was recognized as a breed as recently as 1950. It evolved from the local Klepper (Russian for 'nag') crossed with a variety of illustrious foreign blood and is a long-bodied horse with short legs with almost no feather. Its conformation is good and its nature sweet and energetic. It stands around, or just over, 15 hands high and is usually chestnut, but can also be bay. In 1961 a Toric mare became Absolute Heavy Draught Horse Champion of the USSR. *Not illustrated.*

TRAIT DU NORD

This very gentle French heavy draught horse is also very strong. It stands some 16 hands high and weighs about 1 ton. It is bay, chestnut or roan.

The Trait du Nord is very similar to the Ardennais, though a bit taller and heavier, and is the result of crossing that breed with the Brabant. It is bred in the north-east of France (the same area as the Ardennais) and is sometimes known as the Ardennais du Nord.

TRAKEHNER

Also known as the **East Prussian**, this is a very attractive riding horse standing 16-16.2 hands high.

It looks like a tall, quality show hack and may well be the finest of Germany's saddle horses. It is a spirited horse with tremendous stamina.

The breed dates back to 1732, when King Friedrich Wilhelm I founded the Royal Trakehnen Stud at the easternmost edge of his kingdom. Boundary changes at the end of World War II left most of the 25,000 registered Trakehners in the Soviet bloc and only some 1200 were evacuated to West Germany. Happily, the German Federal Republic has now built up a good stock, while Poland continues to breed the Trakehner with great skill and care.

TURKOMAN

A fine, 'dry' type of desert horse, this is a very ancient breed. It is believed to date back to before the time of Christ and was kept in large numbers by the nomadic Altai herdsmen on the fringe of the Gobi Desert. It still roams semi-wild on the steppes of what is now Iran.

Having both speed and stamina, the Turkoman's principal uses today are for long-distance riding and long-distance racing. Colts are caught and broken in at six months old. They are trained by walking long distances covered with thick blankets to sweat the fat off them. They start racing as yearlings with small boys as jockeys.

The breed has been protected by the Royal Horse Society of Iran since 1971. It stands 15 hands high.

VIATKA

The Viatka is a sturdy, all-purpose pony of typical northern Forest type. It originated in the Viatsky territory of the USSR and is now bred mainly in the Udmurt Autonomous Republic and the Kirov Province.

Very hardy and with a rapid trot, this breed was popular in pre-automobile days for pulling *troika* sledges. It also excels at light agricultural work.

The Viatka stands 13-14 hands high and has good conformation. Typical colours are dun and brown, though it is sometimes roan or grey.

VLADIMIR HEAVY DRAUGHT

This massive agricultural work horse was purpose-bred in Russia during the first half of this century and was officially recognized as a breed in 1946. It appeals to British eyes because there is visible evidence of the Clydesdale and Shire foundation sires which were imported to breed with local mares, though the burliness of Ardennais, Percheron and Suffolk Punch is also apparent.

The breed matures quickly and is a good all-rounder. Standing about 16 hands high, the Vladimir is usually bay with Shire-like white legs and feather and with white face markings.

WALER or AUSTRALIAN STOCK HORSE

Developed in New South Wales – hence its name –
from Dutch and Arab and Thoroughbred stock, the
Waler was a quality saddle horse of about 16 hands
high which became the favourite mount of the
Australian cavalry. More than 12,000 Walers were
sent to fight in the Sinai Desert and Palestine in
World War I and, because of Australian quarantine
laws which do not allow the repatriation of animals,
the survivors were destroyed.

Almost entirely for this reason, the name 'Waler'
no longer exists. Modern 'Walers', bred on nearly
identical lines, are called Australian Stock Horses.

WELSH PONY

Very beautiful and spirited ponies have been running wild in Wales since time out of mind. Records of breeding them go back to the time of Julius Caesar, who, the Welsh Pony Society claims, founded a stud for them at Lake Bala in Merioneddshire and introduced Oriental blood.

The origin of these ponies is uncertain and is larded with romantic myths – understandably, because these ponies are so attractive. For example, translators of the original Latin documents tended to interpret 'Oriental' blood as 'Arab', perhaps because the small Welsh Mountain breed is Araby in type, and there is Arab fire and grace even in the heaviest of Wales's cobs – yet the Arab horse was not one of the twelve breeds known to the Romans.

Arab horses did come into the Welsh line, though obviously not until much later. Within the last few centuries at least two Arabian stallions have run wild with the herds on the Welsh hills. Another debt is owed to the small Thoroughbred stallion, Merlin, a direct descendant of the Darley Arabian, who was loosed in Denbighshire about 200 years ago.

Today's Welsh Ponies range from under 12 hands high to 13.2 hands. Welsh Cobs are larger, and may be as tall as 15.1 hands. All share a common heritage but, because of the range of mountain and moorland habitat to sheltered, fertile valley, and because of the varying needs of the Welsh people, the ponies differ in type and different qualities have been bred for selectively. Outside blood has sometimes been introduced to enhance a special trait.

The following four sections of the Welsh breed have been recognized for nearly 100 years.

Section A: Welsh Mountain Pony

A charming child's pony, standing just under 12 hands high, having an Arab-type head with wide, expressive eyes, dish face and small, pricked ears. Its head and tail are carried gaily and its action is quick and free. The body is short and muscular and the legs fine and hard. Like all Welsh breeds it is sound and sure-footed and hardy. It is very intelligent.

Colours are any except piebald and skewbald, but grey, bay and chestnut are most common.

Section B: Welsh Pony

Standing 12-13.2 hands high, this type excels as a show pony. It is less angular in appearance than the Welsh Mountain and owes a lot to the aforementioned Thoroughbred, Merlin. It looks more like a small hunter than a small hack.

Section B ponies are called 'Merlins' to this day.

Section C: Welsh Pony of Cob Type

Stronger than the Section B, and bred more for harness and light agricultural tasks, this type still does not exceed 13.2 hands high. It is an all-purpose pony, presently used in trekking.

Medieval descriptions required it to be 'fleet of foot, a good jumper, a good swimmer and able to carry a substantial weight on its back'. It has not changed much.

Section D: Welsh Cob
Established as a breed since before the 15th century, this powerful little horse stems from the old Powys

Cob of 800 years ago. Standing 13.2-15.1 hands high, its spirited appearance and airy movement nonetheless demonstrate its relationship with the little Section A Pony.

The intelligent and kind Welsh Cob is so versatile that it has been used for every manner of task. Its agricultural days are over but its countless admirers still think it the best ride-and-drive animal in the world.

WIELKOPOLSKI

A dual-purpose ride-and-drive warmblood from Poland, this breed stands 15.2-16.2 hands high and is a handsome, active horse, noted for its good paces.

It has been developed from two older Polish warmbloods – the Poznan and the Masuren – which in their turn were based on quality imported stock.

WURTTEMBERGER

A medium-weight, tall cob type, standing around 16 hands high, this co-operative German horse has bred true to type for nearly 100 years and succeeds in most of those sports where speed is not required: show jumping, dressage, carriage driving and hunting.

The idea of the Wurttemberg existed long before the horse came into present shape. The stud farm at Marbach, where the horse is principally bred, was founded by Duke Christoph von Wirtemberg in

1573. The Duke intermixed the best horses from neighbouring Hungary and from Turkey. His son, Ludwig, added Andalusians and Neapolitans. Barb and East Friesian horses came later and, at the end of the 19th century, Anglo-Norman and East Prussian blood was introduced.

YAKUT

This is a primeval pony, close under 13 hands high on average but reaching 14 hands or so where climate permits. Few other ponies would survive in the dreadful climate of the Yakut Autonomous Republic, which extends north of the Arctic Circle and includes some of the coldest areas in the Northern Hemisphere. Winter temperatures plummet to -69°C (-92°F), while, in summer, smoke fires are lit to enable the herds to graze in the plague-clouds of mosquitos.

The Yakut is invaluable in every way to humans living in this austere habitat. Apart from saddle, transport and pack work, it also provides milk and meat. *Not illustrated.*

ZEMAITUKA

The Yakut excepted, this is probably the toughest pony to be found anywhere in the world. It lives in inhospitable areas of the USSR and comes from Asiatic Wild Horse ancestry with a touch of Arab desert blood.

The Zemaituka survives on the barest of fodder in the harshest of climatic conditions, yet is still able to cover 64km (40 miles) in a day. It stands 13-14 hands high and its colour, as is to be expected from its ancestry, is usually dun with a dark dorsal stripe.

Glossary of horse terms

Action Describes the movement of the legs at all paces.

Baulky Stubborn. Horse sticks his toes in or swings away from his proper direction.

Cattle-cutting Dividing, or cutting, a cow or group of cattle from a larger group.

Coldblood Term used for draught horses, describing a heavy, stolid sort of horse. Absence of the trace of fiery spirit seen in nearly all lightweight horses and ponies (compare Warmblood).

Colt An entire male horse under four years old.

Conformation Describes the shape of the horse as a whole.

Crupper Strap attached to back of saddle and encircling root of horse's tail, to stop the saddle slipping forward.

Dam Mother.

Feather Long, silky hair on horses' lower legs, sometimes partly covering the feet. Most pronounced in heavy breeds such as the Shires.

Filly A female horse under four years old.

Foal A baby horse under one year old, as colt foal, filly foal.

Entire Uncastrated.

Gait As distinct from *paces*, which include the universal walk, trot, canter and gallop, gaits are extra-special movements, such as the running walk, which are peculiar to a few breeds only.

Gelding A castrated horse or pony.

Hack 1. A lightweight riding horse with gentle manners. 2. 'To go for a hack' means to go for an undemanding ride, usually only walking and trotting but sometimes with a slow canter.

Halfbred A cross between a Thoroughbred and any other sort.

Hands The unit for measuring the height of a horse from the ground to its withers, the highest point of its back at the base of the neck. Horses are traditionally measured in 'handbreadths' rather than inches or centimetres, an average hand being assumed as four inches. Thus a horse 'standing 16 hands high' measures 5ft 4in (or 1.6m) to the top of his withers. 'Standing', in this context, means standing up straight rather than dropping height by resting on one leg.

Hinny Offspring of a horse or pony stallion and a female donkey.

Honest Genuine, in the sense of will honestly try, for example, to jump a fence rather than plan to duck out at the last moment.

Horse 1. Any animal of the genus *Equus* standing more than 14.2 hands high (compare Pony). 2. A stallion aged four or more years.

Kind Much the same meaning as in a human. Heavy horses are notably 'kind' in that they will gently do the bidding of a small child despite their own vastly superior strength.

Light-framed Unsubstantial in appearance, due to slender bone structure.

Mare A female horse or pony aged four years old or more.

Markings Standard types of pattern on the coat. *See Colours and markings, pages 234-5.*

Mealy Descriptive of the pale-coloured muzzles of some animals, notably Exmoor ponies, which look as if they had been dipped in meal.

Mule Offspring of a donkey stallion and a horse or pony mare.

Nuts Concentrated horse feed packed into small cylindrical pieces.

Pacer Descriptive of a trotting racehorse who moves both legs on the same side in unison, as opposed to the diagonal lifting of legs displayed at a normal trot.

Paces The four universal movements of the horse: the walk, trot, canter and gallop. *Note*: Some people, but by no means all, refer to a top-speed gallop, in which the horses's frame flattens out slightly and becomes rigid with his effort, as 'running'.

Paddock A fenced-in area of grassland, in Britain usually smaller than an acre but in other countries can be much larger. Generally denotes post and rail fencing rather than hedging but usage is not precise.

Points 1. The various parts of the horse's body. *See diagram on facing page*. 2. In colour descriptions the mane, tail and most of the legs which mary vary in colour from the main coat.

POINTS OF THE HORSE

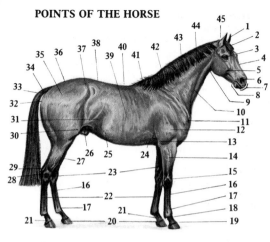

1 Ear	16 Cannon bone	31 Flank
2 Forelock	17 Fetlock joint	32 Point of buttocks
3 Eye	18 Pastern	33 Tail
4 Nose	19 Coronet band	34 Dock
5 Cheek bone	20 Hoof (foot)	35 Hip joint
6 Nostril	21 Heel	36 Croup
7 Muzzle	22 Tendons	37 Point of hip
8 Chin groove	23 Chestnuts	38 Loins
9 Throat	24 Brisket	39 Ribs
10 Jugular groove	25 Belly	40 Back
11 Point of shoulder	26 Sheath	41 Withers
12 Shoulder	27 Gaskin (2nd thigh)	42 Mane
13 Elbow	28 Hock joint	43 Crest
14 Forearm	29 Point of hock	44 Neck
15 Knee	30 Stifle	45 Poll

Pony Any animal of the horse species standing 14.2 hands high or under when mature. Compare Horse.

Prance Jiggle about in an excited manner, often with tiny rears or leaps.

Prepotent Tending to throw offspring of marked family resemblance, sometimes for many generations.

Sickle hocks Hocks which, viewed from the side, are excessively bent at the joint, so that the line from hock to ground angles forwards instead of being vertical. A structural weakness.

Sire Father.

Slippy Describing a slightly-built horse or pony with spontaneous, erratic sideways movement, making it difficult for a rider to stay on board.

Stallion An entire horse or pony aged four years old or more.

Warmblood Thought to contain traces of Oriental ancestry, giving spirit and fire. Almost all lightweight horses and ponies fall into this category.

Weaving A rhythmical fidgeting shift of weight from one forefoot to the other with accompanying weaving motion of head and neck. Stabled horses do it when bored or impatient. Undesirable because it inhibits the horse's rest.

Windsucking Like weaving, a vice of boredom. The horse grabs hold of a bit of wood – usually his stable door or paddock railing – and gulps in air. Highly undesirable in terms of the damage it can do to his fragile respiratory system, and extremely difficult to cure.

Colours and markings

COLOURS

Albino Completely white coat with pink skin and pinkish or blue eyes, which often lack colour (dark-eyed albinos have been developed in the United States).

Appaloosa Spotted horses in several patterns, both light on dark and dark on light. Visible skin is mottled pink. They include:

Blanket or Blagdon Spots on white on loins and quarters only.

Leopard spot Dark spots on white.

Marble A round or oval concentration of lighter or darker spots giving an overall mottled appearance, usually roan.

Raindrop Markings like droplets of water

Snowflake spotted White spots on darker background.

Bay Brown coat with black mane, tail and legs. There are several shades of brown coat though legs, main and tail are always black:

Blood bay Rich horse-chestnut colour.

Bright, or Light, bay Almost chestnut, but with more red than yellow.

Dark bay Similar to black-brown with flanks, muzzle and ribs in main bay colour.

Golden bay Golden red.

Mealy bay Rust colour.

Black Coat colour completely black (except for any white markings) including skin, mane, tail, limbs and muzzle.

Black-Brown All-over black but with muzzle, and occasionally flanks, brown or tan.

Brown Coat colour combining black and chocolate throughout. Muzzle is tan and occasionally there is brown on the flanks.

Chestnut Coat colour of bright, rather carrot red. Skin, muzzle, mane and tail the same colour, though mane and tail may be lighter. In North America **Sorrel** is the general term for a chestnut horse. There are several shades of chestnut:

Dark Chestnut From reddish brown to near-black.

Golden Chestnut Reddish shot with gold.

Light Chestnut Red with a tinge of cream (known as

Sorrel   **Chestnut**   **Liver Chestnut**

mealy), yellow (*lemon*) or of dead sorrel or dock flowers (*sorrel*).

Liver Chestnut Between sand and cooked liver in colour.

Red Chestnut Deep, bright red.

Cream Coat colour of rich cream with pink skin. Mane, tail and muzzle are matching cream or may be silver. Eyes are often pinkish and lack colour.

Dun Coat colour of the following shades but always with black skin and muzzle and sometimes with a dark dorsal stripe from withers to tail, often also with transverse stripes and zebra markings:

Blue Dun Mouse coloured.

Light Dun Lighter mouse.

Silver Dun Oyster colour.

Yellow Dun Light lemon.

Bay   **Brown**   **Black**

229

Gold, Metallic   Golden with a metallic sheen (as in the Akhal-Teké).

Grey   A range of coat shades with a mixture of black and white hairs through the coat. The skin is black except where white markings occur, where it will be pink. All greys tend to be very dark in the young animal and become pale, even white as they age. The basic grey has a grey mane and tail.

Dappled Grey   Small dark circles on a lighter ground, usually more evident in summer.

Flea-bitten Grey   Light grey with brown or reddish hairs freckling throughout.

Iron Grey   With brown hairs spread through the grey.

Blue Roan   **Flea-bitten Grey**   **Dapple Grey**

Rose Grey   With reddish chestnut hairs.

Silver Grey   Nearly white with silver mane and tail.

Steel Grey   Dark grey coat with black mane and tail.

Metallic Gold   see Gold.

Odd-coloured   A coat with a mixture of more than two colours in patches which merge at the edges. Also used for a horse that is not whole coloured.

Palomino   A creamy-golden coat like the colour of a gold coin. Mane and tail are white with only a small proportion of dark or chestnut hairs. There should be no white markings on the body (they are permitted on the legs) and the muzzle is brown or black.

Paint   See *Pinto*

Piebald   Distinct patches of black and white on a black skin in two forms:

Albino   **Appaloosa**   **Leopard Spotted**

231

Strawberry Roan   **Dun**   **Palomino**

Overo White patches extending from the belly upwards. Back, mane and tail usually black. White faces and light coloured eyes common.

Tobiano White from the back downwards but with patches of colour, usually on head, chest, flank and buttocks. White legs common but not white faces.

Pinto North American term embracing both piebald and skewbald.

Roan A coat of solid colour mixed with white on a black skin, variously:

Bay (or Red) Roan Bay or bay brown, so that it has a reddish tinge, with dark mane, tail and muzzle.

Black Roan Black with white and black mane, tail and legs.

Blue Roan Grey and white coat, giving a blue appearance, with dark mane, tail, muzzle and legs.

232

Cream **Piebald** **Skewbald**

Brown Roan Brown and white coat with brown mane, tail, muzzle and legs.

Chestnut (or Strawberry) Roan Chestnut and white, giving a pinkish colour, with chestnut or golden mane, tail, muzzle and legs.

Skewbald A coat splashed with large patches of white or any definite colour except black – usually a mixture of bay/white, chestnut/white or lemon/white. Skin colour varies.

Sorrel North American name for chestnut. Also shade of chestnut.

Spotted see Appaloosa.

MARKINGS

Blaze   Broad white mark down the face.

Donkey Stripe   Same as dorsal stripe.

Dorsal Stripe   Black or dark brown line running along the spine.

Ermine Marks   Black spots on a white background, usually on legs.

Patch   Any large definite irregular area.

Sock   White leg extending upwards from the hoof over the fetlock joint.

Snip   Small white stripe between nostrils.

Star   White mark on the forehead.

Stocking   White leg extending upwards from the hoof to the knee or hock.

Stripe   Thin white mark running down face.

Transverse Stripe   Line across the withers at right-angles.

White Face   Blaze wide enough to cover forehead and eyes, extending over the nose and most or all of the muzzle.

White Pastern (*or Coronet, Fetlock etc*)   A small amount of white covering only the part of the body named.

Zebra stripe   Bar stripes on on upper insides of legs, only seen in primitive breeds.

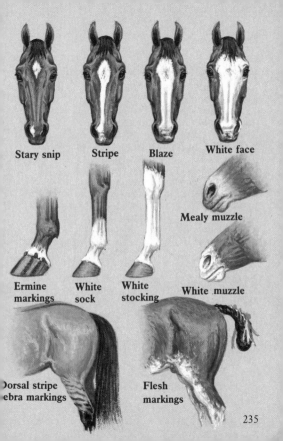

Stary snip

Stripe

Blaze

White face

Mealy muzzle

Ermine markings

White sock

White stocking

White muzzle

Dorsal stripe zebra markings

Flesh markings

235

Index